LETTERS FROM ALASKA:
Hazards and Humor of
Life in Subrrrbia

LETTERS FROM ALASKA

Hazards and Humor of
Life in Subrrrbia

by

Edith C. Rohde

with illustrations by

William D. Berry

THAT NEW PUBLISHING COMPANY
1525 Eielson Street / Fairbanks, Alaska 99701

Library of Congress Catalog Card No. 79-66091

International Standard Book No. 0-918270-04-9

Manufactured in the United States of America

First Printing October 1979

THAT NEW PUBLISHING COMPANY
1525 Eielson St. / Fairbanks, Alaska 99701

with
fondest memories of
William D. Berry
May 20, 1926 to May 14, 1979
We Miss You!

TABLE OF CONTENTS

ACKNOWLEDGEMENTS

These "letters," this book, could not have been written without all the people, *all the people,* who make up my life, every single one of you.

For taking a chance on a woman who wanted to publish her letters in the Fairbanks *Daily News-Miner,* I thank Kent Sturgis, managing editor.

For suggesting that the column become a book I thank Judy Triplehorn, who was serious, and Ernie Line, who was teasing.

For seeing to it that the book came about I thank "Rusty" Walker.

Finally, oceans of appreciation to Stephen Vanek, Jr., for his encouragement and his enthusiastic response to the first reading of "that kind of stuff!" which eventually became the column.

INTRODUCTION

Living in Alaska never made sense to the folks back home. Once we were up here they just kept waiting for us to come to our senses and move back down. Oblivious to their deep-seated conviction that we were not too bright for straying and staying so far afield, I wrote to them regularly with glowing praises of the joys of life in the Far North.

Once I realized that my elaborate explanations of cold, dark winters, life without plumbing and houses that sink into permanently frozen soil were creating suspicions about my sanity rather than respect for my choice of habitat, I switched tactics.

Carefully, cautiously and with some sense of distress at my disloyalty to the myth of the Last Frontier I began poking fun at our winter-dominated, less-than-convenient lifestyle. Instead of trying to deny the dreary aspects of ice fog, the pain of fifty below, the deprivation created by isolation I boasted about it, with a smile.

I painted pretty pictures of digging outhouse holes in soggy mud, being seasick while slinging salmon aboard an undulating gill netter and brushing aside frozen tears while trying to coax a car to start at many minuses below.

It just so happened that my letters were printed weekly on the Northern Life page of the Fairbanks *Daily News-Miner,* and lo and behold, though the lowlanders still didn't quite seem to appreciate our dilemma, the locals embraced the assessment whole-heartedly. Next thing I knew my letters were being sent by people all over town to relatives all over the country in multiple attempts to try to explain why we flourish in Fairbanks, Alaska.

This book was sparked by the encouragement of enthusiastic readers and supportive friends who asked to have "all the columns" clipped out and bundled together to use as a response to that frequent question, "Why do you live in Alaska?"

One of these friends, wildlife artist, sculptor, muralist, illustrator and humanist William D. "Bill" Berry, chose to add illustrations which offered his version of the lifestyle described "so people can see as well as read what we're up against up here."

Here they are, by popular demand, two years of a one-sided correspondence—letters to real people about real situations in a real world that sometimes seems to good to be true.

—Edith C. Rohde
Fairbanks, Alaska
May 1, 1979

I'M LEAVING HERE—
SOON OR EVENTUALLY

June 27, 1977

Dear Mom and Dad,

It really is hard to try to explain why we live here. I know, I know, I told you we'd be right down as soon as we sold the house.

Well, we were trying to get out of this wretched place and move closer to home, but the house didn't sell, the snow melted, the birch leaves burst, the puddles dried up, the weather warmed up, the nights brightened up and it looks as if we won't be down after all.

We jacked up the house! Remember, we live on permafrost. So when the thaw comes the house tends to wobble a bit. The thing is, the ground is frozen, but reacts to heat caused by pressure created by the weight of the house. Some of the permafrost becomes less "perma" due to our weight (not ours, but the house's). Oh dear, that doesn't explain it very well, does it?

Yes, Dad, it does explain why the land was so cheap.

That splendid ski trail that crosses the land in the winter and connects with the 12-mile trail, the 26-mile trail and the Skiathon course turns into a creek in the summer. The water can't sink into frozen earth so it runs off. This is great except we have to wear hip boots to wade, I mean walk, to the outhouse, and it does breed mosquitoes.

The mosquitoes at this time of year are huge and slow and hardly bite at all, just lull us to sleep with their zzzzz. It is always so intriguing to have this slow batch before they breed small, fast, fiesty offspring.

Oh! Back to selling the house, or rather not selling it. Some people seemed to expect running water. I explained that it really isn't any bother to shower at the gym, haul water, collect rain or melt snow. Then I mentioned the convenience of not having to worry about frozen pipes in the winter. Too often I'd find the prospective buyer gazing past me at the visqueen-covered insulation in the ceiling.

It seemed to me to be quite fortunate that the ceiling isn't covered with anything permanent like wood. This way potential buyers see the construction. One fellow noticed the insulation was sagging a bit and gave it a hefty shove before I could warn him. You should have seen his startled expression when the squirrel's supply of dog food fell at his feet.

"That cinches it!" I said convincingly (I hope), "I'm going to close up that squirrel hole, just as soon as I find out when they give birth. I don't want to risk disturbing a young family."

I realize this is going to disturb *my* family, but here goes. We have taken the house off the market. We are going to stay here awhile longer. If only it had sold in the middle of the cold, dark winter, leaving would have been so easy then.

Please don't try to understand. Just figure we're a little bit silly. Think positive. We *will* be down as soon as possible—*for a visit.*

> Love you lots and miss you much,
> Dee

PLASTIC GARDENING

June 12, 1977

Dear Sis,

My fingers are grimy, my shoes smell like manure, my back is stiff and my knees are sore, but oh! Oh, what lovely, even rows and hills of dirt, seedlings and visqueen.

Just in the knick of time. Surely those plants don't know what day it is. Maybe they would grow even if I didn't get them in the ground by June first. Maybe, but I shall never know. I don't have the courage to try. In fact, I don't think I have ever met one brave soul, one innovator who dares set plants into the ground before May 30 or risks the unknown consequences of waiting until after the magic date.

I asked Marilyn, of 29 gardening seasons. "Let me see." She responded. "Late in May, but always by June 1st. Remember one year it did snow May 30th. Ummm. May 31st is a good time." So goes the advice from all sources.

Regimented? No! Dedicated, devoted, drawn by the lure of the dirt. At least that's what we tell ourselves.

Last weekend the rumble of rototillers around the neighborhood resembled an invasion. Rented or borrowed machines advanced across the hill. Surely a general was marshalling his forces. Soil was attacked. It yielded and surrendered. The machines moved on to the next plot of ground. Rumble, rumble, rumble and then hush.

For another year, that noisy night is past and we are left to admire our blanketed gardens.

Somewhere vegetables start out fresh and end up in plastic—limp and pale. A vision of their former selves, they reach us worn and weak from their travels. At our house they start out snuggled in the dirt, covered with warmth and moisture maintaining plastic and end up huge, lush, crisp and fresh. That seems like a nicer order of events.

I recall one year a letter of concern arrived in the midst of the growing season. I was weeding with the sun on my back. Music drifted out from the house. Pausing to nibble a tender baby carrot I read the comments from California. Sympathy was expressed for those of us living in the frozen north during these times of escalating prices.

"It's bad enough down here, but up there where prices are already so high it must be unbearable!"

Groceries? Gracious! With moose on the table, salmon in the smoker, berries ready to be picked, mushrooms in the woods, tomatoes in the greenhouse and salads and vegetables crowding the garden faster then we could pick and eat or process them, I contemplated how much we needed that sympathy.

How could I best explain our plight? Mayonnaise, Margarine . . . what else was on the grocery list this month? Ah! Yes! We traded moose meat for fresh eggs from the family down the road, but we had to buy our milk from the store and milk is very expensive.

Easily, that evening with a mug of home brew in hand, I answered the letter with explanations of the hardships of life in Alaska.

> Miss you much. More later,
> Big Sis

LIGHT-ALL-NIGHT
BEATS DARK-ALL-DAY

June 20, 1977

Dear Sharron and Will,

It's almost midnight and as I write this the sky to the north is ablaze with the most magnificent sunset you can imagine. If there is one part of Alaska that I cannot resist, it is light-all-night. Dark-all-day doesn't do a thing for me, but light-all-night is worth stumbling around in December.

I am a born skeptic. My garden suffers because I keep digging up the seeds to see if they really are doing anything down under there where I can't see them. When Young Son tells me he's cleaned his room and is headed off, I'm the kind of mother

18

who checks under the bed and the floor of the closet before I tell him to go play.

This means that when we first came to Alaska, each summer at least once, and often twice, I stayed up until morning to find out if it really does stay light all night long. Fact is, you can go to bed very late and get up very early, but unless you don't shut your eyes at all how are you going to know for sure?

I remember the summer my dad was up here in June and kept watching the newspaper reports of how many minutes of daylight we had. Finally he asked, "When do the minutes of darkness happen? I've been awake at all hours and haven't seen the dark yet."

Technically the sun sets, but it doesn't go far enough below the horizon to give us darkness. So it really does stay light all night. It's fantastic!

The summer I worked nights as a janitor, I got paid to stay awake. I organized my schedule so that between sunset (11 p.m.) and sunrise (1 a.m.) I could clean all the north facing rooms. I dusted desks and vacuumed floors while facing the windows and watching the brilliant glowing sky. It was a truly lovely job.

Before coming to Alaska I'd heard about the midnight sun, but like so much you hear about this great state I assumed the stories were grossly exaggerated.

I remember the first time the daylight confused me. In what seemed like the middle of a lively party for which I was the hostess the guests began to say good night. I was distressed by their departure and insisted, "You can't leave so soon. It isn't even dark yet."

Sleepily, with an indulgent smile, a friend shook her head and said, "Edee, it's 3 a.m. and it's not going to get dark for several months. We can't stay that long."

About a week later the children went out to play after dinner and didn't come back. Now, my kids are remiss about a lot of things, but they know I get hysterical when they don't come home on time. So, of course, I knew instantaneously that they had been abducted.

By the time I found them (happily playing in the playground) I was fuming. They didn't understand my distress. The rule had always been to come home when the street lights came on and the lights were not lit, and wouldn't be for several months.

Enough reminiscing. Must write to my folks. Come to think of it, I'll probably wait up for the sun to rise. Just to make sure.

Greetings from the glowing Northland,
Dee

MAKING SPACE

July 4, 1977

Dear Auntie Mae and Uncle Harve,

Hi! Sorry it's been so long since I've written. This will be a long overdue explanation about housing up here.

When we first arrived in Fairbanks the woman who was moving out of the apartment we were moving into invited me to lunch at her just-built home. With no difficulty, I found the correct house, because it had been described as "tar-paper covered, the siding isn't up yet." Not an apology, merely a useful bit of identifying information.

The door was shiny white with inset diamond shaped windows. The doorbell resounded splendidly throughout the house. My hostess opened her lovely new front door, and to my astonishment (and confusion) I was gazing at the inside of the outside of the house. I'd just stepped into my first *shell*.

She showed me from "room" to "room" with pride, never realizing (I hope) how surprised I was to see her French provincial bedroom set next to the unhung sheetrock and unplumbed bathtub. We were careful not to step through any "walls." We used the designated door jams. Etiquette seemed to require such courtesy.

As you know, we adapted quickly to Alaskan living and soon realized that affordable housing would have to be do-it-yourself, a step at a time. Thus our introduction to log peeling.

If blisters and sore muscles don't count, over the years the children and I have managed to peel thousands of linear feet of

20

dead trees without injury. Some of the injuries I feared were those that might be caused by committing mayhem while trying to enforce the four-logs-per-day rule.

"That's your problem, Mother. You may drive yourself, if you choose, but don't expect me to do the same." The child suffered no bruises, but she did come to realize that it was indeed her problem too.

"Oh, I can't. I'm too tired." Explained Young Son, the natural gold bricker.

"Four logs before you catch the school bus!" I insisted. It was easy to be a firm parent when my arms ached too much to take another turn.

"I'll walk." He was too tired to peel four logs, but not too tired to walk five miles to school.

The complaints and hassles were exhausting, but the children proved that they could and would do four logs per day. Four for them, then perhaps 8 for me, or 12.

Twelve proved unwise, because for three days after that I was unable to lift the drawknife (log peeling implement).

The children grew and so did the house. The next time it was log peeling time not much supervision was necessary. I peeled at my leisure and the children governed themselves and each other. At one point I recall hearing distinct noises of peer pressure such as:

"You are not done!!! I peeled half that log myself, before dinner and you can't claim it! Come right back here this minute or else!"

There was a point where I began to worry that we might not get through that project without injury. Had better sign off. There is always ever so much to do to spiffy up the space we have created.

Your loving niece,
Edith C.

WOES OF A SEASICK
SALMON FISHERONE

July 11, 1977

Dear Jerry,

You asked about fishing in Alaska. The best I can do is describe my summer as a licensed commercial fisher*man*. I chose fishing for the freedom, fresh air and autonomy. Boy was I naive. What I experienced instead was a rigorous salty education. Let me tell you about the operation.

Up here we have limited entry, which means that only certain people can fish. So first of all I had to find someone to fish with who had a permit to fish. The next effort was readying the boat for the water: scraping, sanding, painting, etc. This appears to be a never-ending chore that is merely declared done when the season opens.

What a thrill to watch an enormous crane dangle a 32 foot bright and shiny vessel high up over the water and carefully set it down with nary a splash! It floated! (Exhale.) After that big moment the real work began.

There were certain days when fishing was allowed, certain hours, certain areas. It was essential to listen to the radio, because the rules had a habit of changing all of a sudden.

We fished in Ninilchik, Cook Inlet, where a boat can only go in or out of the harbor at a convenient hour. We would get up in the middle of the night, take the boat out of the harbor, anchor up and go back to sleep on board or go to the fishing grounds and sleep there.

As near as I can determine, where we slept depended mainly on how tired the captain was.

No matter when we napped, at 6 a.m. sharp we were on deck to drop in the gill net. Watching the action on all the boats around, you would think there was a giant timeclock in the sky.

Once the net was in a reasonably straight line the required number of feet from the next boat's gear, we waited for indications that there were fish. The trailing tail of hundreds of feet of large meshed net hangs perpendicular to the surface of the water, suspended by floats. The salmon can't see it (I guess), swim into it, get caught by their gills and thrash around. So bobbing corks (floats) or impatient crew members signal that it's time to reel aboard the net.

By scooping fingers into the gills, you work the fish backwards out of the net, avoiding teeth and tail. Hopefully a good last shake releases the creature. Plop! You chase it across the slimy deck. Grab it. Toss it down the chute into the hold and try not to notice how many your buddy had deftly plucked and tossed while you were floundering.

No, I didn't mind the hours, the blood and slime, the smell or being continually cold and wet. Yes, I did get seasick, but not on choppy, rough and scary days. Only when the water was calm and the boat heaved up and down. I had to give up taking seasick pills because they gave me courage enough to yell back at the captain. He didn't like that.

There is evidently no such thing as enough fish. We never stopped flinging out that net and pulling it back in until the buzzer sounded. (There really wasn't a buzzer, it just felt that way.)

When time was up we'd steam back to the tender and wait in line for a few hours to sell the fish. Always we hoped there would be an extra period scheduled so we could get more fish. Also we hoped there wouldn't be so we could get some rest, some groceries and some boat maintenance done.

That was definitely not my idea of a relaxing vacation, but in all honesty, in spite of all the trauma and travail, I wouldn't swap that summer for all the fish in the ocean.

Good luck with your marine plans, whatever they may be.

Landlubber me,
Edee

EMISSARIES FROM OUTER STATE

July 18, 1977

To My Favorite Families of the San Francisco Bay Area,

The first Alaskans I ever met were staying in Colorado for a school year. They were fascinating people, totally miserable, lonely and homesick. All they could talk about was Alaska. That was fine with us because what they had to say was interesting.

He was a scientist who studied, among other things, the aurora borealis. Until then I had believed the Northern Lights were mythical. They're not. He told me more about them than I could understand. He had built their large log home, plus two smaller cabins. How fine—built their home and much of the furniture in it!

He had climbed various mountains, was a serious musician, an excellent cross-country skier and a good dancer.

She was a silver jeweler. She made most of the family clothing, including their parkas and mukluks. Parkas, we learned, are a kind of heavyduty jacket necessitated by the extreme cold and mukluks are foot gear. Imagine making jackets and boots!

She fed her family from their garden in summer (A garden in Alaska?!) and froze and canned the surplus for the winter. She picked berries from a sunny hillside, made syrup and juice concentrates as well as jam. She was making a room-sized latch hook rug for the livingroom. As an attentive hostess and a gracious guest she had a talent for making others comfortable.

They spoke of holidays shared with friends, of saunas, sledding parties, canoe trips, moose hunting, salmon fishing, ice skating, brilliant fall foliage, the crispness of winter cold, a sudden burst of spring and the joy of midnight sunlit skies.

We enjoyed their company for the few months we all spent in Colorado. When we were due to return to California, reluctantly, we envied their eagerness as they headed for the ferry to go home to that faraway place we could hardly imagine.

Fascinating creatures from an outer state!

Many months later a man from Alaska called on us. On some scientific expedition he was headed from the North Pole to the South Pole. Our friends had told him we were people he ought to stop and see. He echoed the theme we had heard before.

"It's the people! There is a greater concentration of warm, caring, energetic, talented, creative, charming people in Alaska than anywhere else. Imagine a social survival of the fittest."

Less than a year after listening to his yarns about raft races and bush pilots we were picking blueberries in the marshes of the northland. Once we experienced the warmth and openness of everyone who welcomed us to our new state we better understood the loneliness of Alaskans who spend time elsewhere.

The first Alaskans we ever met are still our dear friends, and now neighbors. (In Alaskan terms that means we all live in the same general area not too many miles apart.) We suspect their sabbatical cast them as emissaries on a secret mission to lure unknowing fellow Alaskans to their true home. We are not the only ones they Pied Pipered to the north.

This letter is offered as an introduction and perhaps a warning. Today those two are headed to your area for a few months. We'll miss them, but we also miss you. We've given them your name and address and telephone number. We've asked them to do their best.

Hope to see you soon. Up here where you belong.

As ever,
Edee

479-CLICK

July 25, 1977

Hi Neighbor!

Have you tried to call across town lately? I'm serious. The kids' dad works at the University and I work downtown. To make a simple call to say, remember to pick up Young Son, takes two days and a court order.

When we first arrived in Fairbanks, years ago, I sincerely

25

believed that there was no operator, information or time service here. I never received an answer when I called those numbers so I decided this was a small town trying to look big and they just listed those numbers in the phone book for prestige.

We were here two years before I reached the operator, and then we got disconnected. Eventually she did give me the magic number: four oh. Do you remember 4-0? Those were the days.

It was listed as dialing assistance, but the title was unimportant. What mattered was that someone answered at 4-0. You could try to place a call indefinitely, dial 4-0 and *she* could make a connection for you. The Fairbanks connection.

She was magic. She had the goods on someone. That wasn't all. She would tell you what time it was, whether or not she thought it was going to rain and when the grocery store closed. She was a real person.

One nice thing about our primitive phone system though. Each phone call has a sense of urgency about it. Having successfully reached the number you have been dialing all week you feel compelled to say everything there is to say in case you never get through again.

When someone says, "Oh, I'm *so* glad you called" you know they really mean it.

Once I had to co-sign a contract for a business phone guaranteeing payment no matter who used the phone. I facetiously suggested they insert a paragraph promising the phone company would guarantee service. The lady in the office said, urgently, "Oh, but we couldn't do that!"

Yes, lady, I know.

During the pipeline days I kind of liked the phone problems. No matter what you dialed you got a busy signal. Saved a lot of time. My phone got to the point that it gave a busy signal before I lifted the receiver. Saved money too. I traveled outside to visit my family on money saved by not being able to reach them by phone.

I miss the pipeline conversations. Talked to a friend at Prudhoe one day while a guy from Franklin Bluffs quarrelled with his wife in Florida. Someone calling California from Anchorage cut in. We insisted he hang up until the four of us were through with the circuit. We were able to help solve the

Franklin-Florida couple's problem, but ended up quarrelling terribly about denying a fellow-Alaskan use of the hard-won line.

This started out as a note to say, sorry I missed you when you stopped by. Thank you for the invitation. We'd love to come to dinner. No, our number has not been changed. Yes, we do have your number. Tried to get you 4 times yesterday and 7 the day before.

Leave another note on the door, it's easier.

Edee

HELP!
WE'RE BEING MALLED TO DEATH

August 1, 1977

Dear Judy,

I know how much you miss Alaska, but believe me when it comes to shopping, you got out of town in time. We are being malled to death.

Remember the time you and I took our girls to get dresses? It took us fifteen minutes to determine there were no dresses anywhere in their sizes. The girls settled for candy bars with the logic that soon it would be too cold for dresses anyway. As I recall they wanted ice cream cones, but there was no place in town that sold them.

Saying no was easy. There wasn't any other possibility. Living here was economical. Prices were out of sight, but merchandise was also. Out of sight, out of mind and no money out of the pocket.

Shopping these days is awful—economically. One big problem is that you are apt to find something to buy. First, you have to decide just where to go. There is a mall at the top of town, at the bottom, to the east, to the west and a couple of others I've not been able to find yet.

You know me. Once I've found something I want, I feel duty bound to check out similar stores to make certain the purchase is sensible. Gas used traveling from one shopping area to the next is a whole new expense.

I sort of enjoyed things the way they were. I could shop to my heart's content and never find a thing that fit or was the right color. Happily, I would return home with nothing, satisfied that I'd shopped wisely and saved.

Catalogue shopping always ended up being economical for us. The children and I would pour over numerous calalogues, place a large order and eagerly await arrival of our purchases.

After weeks had trudged by I would trace the missing merchandise and inevitably—instant economy! Either the order had gotten lost, the item was discontinued or the child had outgrown the garment by the time it arrived.

One thing that really worries me is that the reasons for going south are diminishing. Traveling outside to get some sun or to visit relatives always seemed so frivilous. I found it conscience soothing to rationalize that I needed to pick up underwear.

Now instead of going 3000 miles to shop you can walk past the eggs and cheese and find whatever you need. Takes some of the adventure out of living here.

Another problem with the malls is that they're fattening. Dieting was easier in the days when there was no place to get good candy or hard ice cream.

However, some things remain constant. Suppliers still send us everything that doesn't sell any place else. No matter how many stores there are you can rest assured that when one of them is out of safety pins they all are. I'd love to meet the man down there who decides what we can do without.

> Regards from the distant north,
> Edee

OH MY ACHING BACK!

August 8, 1977

Dear Sharron and Will,

For ten days I have had a horrendous, agonizing backache. This is the third time in four months that for no apparent reason I have developed a totally debilitating pain. Not only that, it hurts.

The first two times I toughed it out, but this time I decided to go to a doctor. He had me X-rayed, examined me, prescribed pills and heat therapy and $133.00 later told me, "You have a very bad backache."

Somehow it hurt less before.

"Have you ever done anything to injure your back?" He asked.

"No. I've shoveled snow, chopped wood, lifted logs, carried 5 gallon jugs of water, pushed cars out of ditches, pulled halibut lines, dug outhouse holes, helped place dog houses on top of VW buses, boogied all night, pewed salmon, paddled canoes, rowed skiffs, leaned over little people hours at a time, pick-axed gravel piles and done plenty of dishes in a sink too low, but I've never done anything to injure my back."

"What were you doing when this happened the first time?"

"Driving a bus up the Alaska Highway."

"You know that can cause injury." He cautioned.

"Yes, I know—frostbite, dust-blindness, bottom numbness, mental anguish, emotional insecurity, temporary insanity, boredom and whiplash." I think the pain was making me less than polite.

The pills he prescribed made me groggy. They numbed my touch, mellowed my vision, accentuated sounds, tastes and smells and allowed me to completely concentrate on the nuances of the pain. With a little effort and some eloquence I could have written an elegy to the pain, except it was not deadened one bit.

However, all things have a bright side. I met a lot of nice people as I inched along from place to place. Strangers walked up to me with expressions of concern born of experience and offered sympathy and advice. I met more people who really understood what I was going through in those days I was hobbling along grimacing than I have in my entire life.

Some of the offers I received for therapeutic treatment aren't repeatable, but trust me when I say that everyone has his or her idea of an ideal cure for a pain in the back.

Then one day I found this book about backaches. The author/doctor starts off by describing the backache sufferer. Now I don't know if he has been reading my mail or had my phone tapped, but it sounds as if he definitely knows who I am.

According to him, I *improperly* sit, stand, walk, lift and drive. Also I sleep in the worst possible position.

This doctor/author claims that if I change all my postures, my attitude toward life and my wardrobe; plus run or swim daily and do 8 or 10 exercises twice a day I shall never suffer again. I'll try anything once. Very carefully, but consistently, I adopted his regime.

Now, in addition to my backache, I am uncomfortable due to new muscles in use, exhausted due to an extensive exercise program and in debt. If the plan doesn't work I figure I'll sue him for breach of promise and invasion of privacy.

Cheerio, as I write from the strangest position you can imagine.

Dee

IT'S FAIRTIME!

August 15, 1977

Dear Sis,

Golly, how I wish I could package the spirit of our Fair and send it down to you to brighten up your day.

A week ago I walked the empty Fairgrounds, just me, the crunch of gravel, a couple of electricians and the weather-worn booths and buildings.

As if by magic, this Wednesday the Fairgrounds comes alive. Imagine running children, droning carnies, voices boomed over loudspeakers, music bouncing from bandstand and midway, animated conversations, ferris wheel, cotton candy, excitement in the air, people everywhere, concentrated happenings, sights, smells and sounds.

Add smiling politicians shaking hands and handing out ballons, salespeople offering everything from camping vans to handmade jewelry, midway games of skill and rides that thrill, exquisite exhibits of lovely needlework, the biggest vegetables you ever saw, tasty baked goods, and sparkly jars of jams and jellies.

The days are dotted with parades, entertainers, clowns, bag pipes, pie and pancake eating contests. In the Timber Contest men and women swing axes and chain saws and draw knives. Blue ribbon cooks in the Bake Off create masterpieces before your very eyes. Seamstresses model their own creations in a Fashion Show. Samson and Delilahs demonstrate their strength and skill. There are shows for choosing the Valley's finest artwork, loveliest flowers, favorite pets, best talent and bouncingest babies.

Pungent smells and mingling sounds of pigs, poultry, goats, sheep and cows surround the livestock area. Horsepeople dressed elegantly ride gracefully through their paces. Youngsters feed, pet and brush ponies and lambs.

Tuesday is Exhibit Day. We will arrive selfconsciously to enter those examples of our talents of which we are most proud. Booth decorators will be bustling about with hammer, nails, paint brushes, crepe paper and thumbtacks.

Wednesday through Sunday the Fair lives. Every flower box and thumb tack is in place. We'll stand in the long restless line, buy our tickets, enter the gate and head for the area where our entries wait. What did the judges think of our offerings? We will admire the clever decoration of the division. Notice the extremely well done competition and wonder. Where is mine?

Some spot the ribbon and glow with the pleasure of recognition, of approval. Some feel the disappointment of knowing that, after all, mine was good, but others' were better.

The only thing more fun than attending the Fair is being involved in it. For five days the Fair is the world for booth holders, division superintendents, judges, exhibit tenders, Fairguides and scores of helpers.

Then late Sunday night, prize money tucked away, treasured exhibits clutched in hand, we walk through the emptying grounds. Torn tinsel flutters in the breeze, vacant tents snap in the darkness, voices echo against deserted buildings.

The spell is broken. Something underfoot rattles across the gravel. Was it an empty pop can or Cinderella's slipper?

Until next time,
Your loving sister

GONE—ALL GONE

August 22, 1977

Dear Auntie Carolyn and Uncle George,

One sunlit midnight in June, my drive home was interrupted by a long train traveling south across the highway. The train was covered with bulldozers, dump trucks, front loaders, steam rollers and all kinds of huge, dirty, greasy heavy equipment whose names I do not know. No people present, just an exodus of giant machines.

Men wearing pointy-toed boots, broad-brimmed hats and fading tans no longer crowd our downtown streets. In the super market groups of men discussing what's easiest and fastest to cook don't outnumber mothers pushing toddler-laden shopping carts any more.

Those changes I had experienced and hardly noticed, but yesterday the truth hit home. *They* had gone! The foreigners, the occupation forces (to use Carl Benson's apt expression), have dwindled to a manageable few. This hit me because of a shocking experience.

I didn't try to trick her. I wasn't being sneaky. I was preoccupied. I was talking to a friend. In a super market I rarely frequent, a clerk I have never seen before cashed my check. Cashed

© 1979 W. D. Berry

my check, for several dollars over the amount of purchase, without demanding that I show any identification.

I was stunned. I assumed it was an error. I considered shoving my drivers license, gas credit card, social security number and car registration under her nose and insisting, "Here! You can't just take a check for $11.97 without verifying my identity. What sort of an irresponsible act is that?"

Well, I didn't want the poor girl to lose her job over a check that I knew full well was covered. So I quietly tiptoed out of the building and leaned breathlessly against the wall to consider the significance of what had happened.

Then I got an idea. I would go back into the store and try again, just to see if she would make the same mistake twice. The trouble was, I didn't need another sack of cat food. Not only that, my bank balance was getting low and the day was getting late. Perhaps, she is having a bad day, I thought. She'll probably never let it happen again. I dismissed the problem and went home to feed the cat.

A few days later, in a different store. I found myself intentionally moving slowly when reaching for my packet full of identifying information. Sure enough! Before I could produce my credentials she was smiling her "How are you today?" to the next costumer.

What an absolute marvel! What freedom! It has been years, literally years, since I cashed a check without wondering if I was really me. A couple of years ago the bank required 2 pieces of ID before allowing me to make a deposit into my own account, now we've come to this.

We are recognizable! The crowd has thinned. The pace has slowed. Once again we know who we are. Who are we? The same clerks, waitresses, delivery people, teachers, lawyers and so forth that we always were, working at the same jobs.

How nice to be alone together again. Welcome to those who joined us along the way! We have weathered an historic event and we are all still alive and well and living in Alaska, our own hometown.

Write soon,
Edee

"THE" HIGHWAY

August 29, 1977

Dear Jay,

You wanted to know about the highway. What an experience! You know how adamantly opposed everyone was to my driving into Mexico. Well, little did they realize that the real dangers lay to the north, rather than the south.

Dusty cars pulling into town these days cause me to shudder. I am amazed that people wear bumper stickers admitting they've done it. I only refer to the trip when pressed about traumatic experiences I'd rather forget.

Beautiful! Oh, I've no quarrel with that. When you can see through the pitted, grime-covered windshield and the flying dust, gravel and snow, it is 1523 miles of beautiful. Over and over and over again.

I sympathize with those who've driven it in mud and heat, but I do believe when temperatures drop below zero there is a bit more drama to the trek. Due to the snow, there is also less road—on the right hand side and the left hand side, but not at the beginning or the end.

My vehicle, you realize, was a 27 1/2 foot, 29 passenger bus, a homemade camper. It has no circulating heater for warming up the engine, but that was no problem, because there wasn't any place to plug one in anyway. Since we traveled when it was super cold, I woke up every 3 to 4 hours during the night to start the engine. This created the vague impression that I was driving in my sleep.

The highway wasn't as frightening as the traffic. Competition both directions for that one well-worn set of tire tracks that obviously work makes kamikaze flights seem tame. Huge barreling bombs roar toward you filling the entire road with a cloud of flying snow and/or dust and gravel.

You hold your breath, grip the steering wheel firmly and force yourself to keep your eyes open and remain on the road. Everytime the cloud settled I was amazed to discover we were still alive. 1523 miles of terror.

The Alaska Highway is probably the best captioned road there is. Highway maintenance consists of identifying the problem. Signs announce: bad curve, bump ahead, damaged pavement, deep hole, etc. all along the way. How naughty does a curve have to be to be labeled "bad?"

We planned our driving hours so as to stop each night near a business establishment. Misery loves company. Inevitably, when we reached our destination it was deserted—closed for the winter. I resisted the urge to deface countless snow-covered "Welcome Campers" and "Hot Showers" signs.

Along the way the beauty is in the people as much as the scenery: the man in Wonowon who defrosted the engine and recharged the battery; the people in Ft. Nelson who fixed the propane leak in the wee hours of the night; the librarian at Watson Lake who stayed open late for us (There isn't a whole lot to do in Watson Late in the evening.); the two boys who changed the tire at Teslin; the family at Johnson's Crossing who allowed us to park in their yard; the couple from Arkansas that we pulled out of a ditch.

The Northland is a small town. We were 504 miles from home the first time we heard, "Welcome back! How was the trip to Mexico? Bet it's nice to be headed home again." from some roadhouse owners who remembered chatting with us on our way south.

Yes, it is just as bad as you've heard. Yes, you ought to do it anyway, at least once. Come on up. The welcome mat is out. Oh, and on the way, tell the French man at the Beaver Creek Chevron hello for me. Tell him I'll stop by again before too long.

Edee

IT'S THE BERRIES

September 5, 1977

Dear Grandma and Grandpa Turner,

We first arrived in Alaska at this time of year. We were crowded in with another family while waiting for our duplex to be vacated. So when our hostess suggested we go berry picking it sounded like a clever, quaint way to get us all out of the house for a frolic. We packed a picnic basket and a car full of children and drove up to one of the highest spots around. There we met another family with a car full of children and we all tumbled out at a wide spot in the road. Little children ran off over the hillside.

The other two mothers and the older children almost immediately crouched over, lowered their heads and began slowly and silently creeping through the scrubby brush.

At a polite distance I followed my hostess, venturing a gentle throat clearing to catch her attention, but she seemed possessed. With only their example to guide me, I clutched a wire-handled coffee can in hand and began to search for something to pluck.

Sure enough there were tiny round red things hovering near the ground. Though they were a bit hard and not too plentiful, I figured these must be what my friends were looking for. Having nothing better to do, I decided to help. I crouched down popped a few in the can, a few in my mouth and looked up to make sure this wasn't a joke. (They didn't taste too great.)

Off in the distance stretched an incredible, snow-covered mountain range, jagged and grand; by shifting slightly I could see the entire town of Fairbanks spread out and the Tanana River winding endlessly through the valley. With a slight turn of my head my gaze met brilliant hillsides splashed with fall foliage and rolling hills of deep spruce green. The sky was bright blue and clouds drifted overhead.

What a magnificent view! We seemed to be on top of the world, to be able to see everywhere. Correction. *I* seemed to be able to see. The long time Alaskans had their heads in the bushes. They moved about like hungry bears systematically stripping each bush. This wasn't an excuse to get out of the house! They were really picking berries!

During the years since then, I have picked blueberries in the rain, ankle-deep in a swamp, with frozen fingers and toes and even when scared to death because I knew somewhere in the bushes was a moose competing for the spoils.

I have picked rosehips, though I didn't know what to do with them; highbush cranberries, though I don't like them; and crowberries because they were there. I have picked raspberries until I was stuffed, scratched and bleeding. In good years I have difficulty making it from the house to the car because of the bright spots on the path crying out to be gathered.

Given the company I keep, I cannot consider myself a berry picker. I do not set aside certain weeks of the year during which all other activities cease. I do not fib to others about where the berries are best this year. I do not maintain a supply of pails, pans, pants and shoes specific to each berry. I do not return year after year to the same spot, pick it clean and shake the bushes to foster growth for next year. In short, I'm an amateur.

I had better sign off, because I do feel guilty that I'm sitting here writing to you rather than out crawling through the bushes.

Yours in berry juice,
Edee

HARVEST TIME

September 12, 1977

Dear Mom and Dad,

Maybe there are people who harvest their garden with a clear conscience when it is convenient for them. Maybe some systematic individuals say, "I'll freeze the broccoli and cauliflower this weekend, the snow peas Monday, etc." Maybe there are a few who don't try to use every last day of our limited growing season, but I never met them.

The gardeners I know suffer from what I call: instant frozen-vegetables-if-you-don't-watch-out.

We spend a lot of time listening to weather reports and reading thermometers, a lot of time trying to remember how the weather went last fall and that other year that was similar to this one, and a lot of time on the phone seeking reassurance that someone else is going to tough it out just one more night.

Then suddenly—action! Freeze until the freezer bulges, can until you run out of jars and storage space, eat as much and often as possible, pickle more things than imaginable, hang the tomato plants with hopes the green will glimmer red, sauerkraut the cabbage, cellar the roots—but there are limits. (Never, it seems, to the supply.)

Generosity is permissable, even admirable, but it is difficult to find a friend who isn't also trying to get rid of a surplus of lettuce, mustard spinach and radishes.

How can a plot of so few square feet, how can those tiny plants and seeds you pressed into the dirt just three months ago, overrun the kitchen, the pantry, the freezer and your daily schedule?

39

I can never waste so much as a squash blossom. My family was relieved when I learned that the brussel sprout plant stalk can be plowed under to enrich the soil. Middle Child was convinced I was going to boil it up and serve it with butter.

Inevitably at some point amid the steam of sterilizing jars, blanching and boiling I lose sight of what it's all about. I begin to think: Who will know if I don't strip that last pea plant? What will really happen if I leave a few of the summer squash to rot under a leaf? Does some giant garden monster roam the area checking to see if we've pulled up all the parsley? If I miss a stem of rhubarb, will it really haunt my dreams? Will my family suffer for want of that piece of pie?

What causes this compulsion? It could be related to "finish your vegetables all gone" or "a job worth doing is worth doing well." A more likely motive is my deep-seated frugality. Given the price of produce, how can I allow one leaf of green to wilt in that rabbit-fenced treasure trove of vitamins?

Figuring up the time used nursing seedlings, weeding, watering and processing the product; adding the costs of seeds, fertilizer (natural, naturally) and replacing knee-worn jeans, I've decided we can't afford to *eat* those vegetables. We must bank them.

Oops! Must take the zucchini bread out of the oven.

> Catch you later,
> Dee

BLUEBERRIES OR MOOSE?

September 15, 1977

Dear Chris and Tom, Cindy and Jennifer,

I've never been moose hunting, but that doesn't mean I know nothing about it. I consider myself a veteran of six successful hunts. I can describe where each animal was sited, how he was stalked, the moment of the kill and every step of the trek back to camp with the beast as a burden. I listen carefully.

I can recount the smell of breakfast cooking on the fire, the brilliance of the tundra, and the thrill of hearing the mountainside hush pierced by the whine of a long overdue plane.

If these hunters didn't regularly return with game I think I'd suspect them of going off for rest and recreation. I know of a man who usually returns with blueberries instead of moose, of a group that one year brought home only a tiny puppy (They named it Moose.) and of a hunting party that's standard accomplishment is horrendous hangovers.

The least successful year our hunters ever had was the year they came close to not returning at all.

They are safety conscious. They are cautious to a fault. They gathered mushrooms to garnish their omelette and almost added their own demise to that of their already quartered moose. (Sportsmen to the core, they worried in their moments of retching and pain about the fate of the moose carcass in the event that they didn't survive.)

A successful hunt has three stages. Number one is the Preparation: prowling around in the basement, garage, storage shed and neighborhood to locate all the gear necessary for the expedition. Number two is the Pursuit: roaming the countryside to track down the victim. Number three is the Aftermath.

The Aftermath is the difficult part, it begins with trying to find the best way to get the beast to transportation and civilization. Once that major and essential accomplishment is taken care of there is the quest for a safe, cat and dog-free, flyless place to hand 600 to 1000 lbs. of edible animal.

Then off to tramp through town in search of the right kind of meat grinder to borrow, buy or rent; pound the pavement for the store with a sufficient supply of suet to suit the needs of the household; find enough butcher wrap, freezer tape, marking pens and sharp knives; relocate that special sausage recipe and remember who borrowed the meat saw last.

It's necessary to lure in enough willing hands to complete the task before time and patience run out; locate and prepare counter space and table tops to work on; comb the hills for pans and large bowls to place the bloody chunks in and commandeer extra room in a freezer somewhere.

The memory of the hunt lingers long, but months later,

frozen package in hand, a new adventure arises. What does 5RS4ToVs mean in the code of 9-76? Will this be steaks or dog scraps? How can I make top sirloin taste like chicken? Speaking of which, I'd better sign off and go fix dinner. How does roast moose beef and broccoli sound?

Write someday. O. K.?
Dee

BLISTER BLUES

September 26, 1977

Dear Sharron and Will,

Again I didn't do it. For eight years in a row I haven't done it, but this year I don't feel guilty. This year I didn't try to kid myself at any point. I didn't tell me that I ought to or that I might. I didn't start out and give up. In fact, I almost didn't show up at all, but at the last minute I couldn't resist.

Last Saturday morning, I turned out with about 600 other crazy people who got up early, skipped cartoons, dressed appropriately, just barely took time for a brisk cup of whatever and milled around outside the gym waiting to hear a gun go off.

Our magnificent marathon strikes again.

About 200 of those people, wearing huge numbers on their bodies like protective armor, took off like a shot running up the hill. Now, if the gun was aimed at those bobbing numbers I could understand their motivation, but they were just running off to be running.

I can't really get too fired up about running to be running. I can understand running a few miles a day for exercise or to keep in shape or to feel noble or to keep from weighing 200 lbs. (I can't imagine doing it, but I can grasp the idea.) Running, mind you, *running*, 26 miles 385 yards just to be running I do not comprehend.

The rest of those people (minus me) set out to see if they could walk those same 26 miles 385 yards in a sensible amount of time. I ask you now, what is sensible about walking 26 miles? The first 12 of those 26 are uphill and the thermometer up here is within nodding distance of 32° these days. Not exactly conditions calculated to foster a casual stroll.

Reluctantly, I confess that I have been tempted. That first year we were here a marathon seemed like such an exciting, challenging, spirited thing to do. What a delightful way, I thought, to enjoy the crispness of fall in the air, to see the countryside awash with brilliant colors and to enjoy the musky odor of high bush cranberries.

What I remember of that event is the smell of sweaty bodies, the air full of moans and complaints and the sight of the limping fellow-sufferer ahead of me, not so close that I could pass, but definitely obstructing my view.

I recall the blisters, the bite of backpack straps, the bulge of the extra sweater on my hip, and the almost immediate realization that I wasn't going to get there.

What keeps those other hikers going? They chat among themselves, they sing, they ponder and enjoy the day, but eventually the brain numbs as much as the body. In other years I've driven the end of the course searching for people who needed to be picked up. Faces are blank, movement sluggish, motion minimal—forward ever forward. I don't understand, but I do admire them.

There is one sweet bit of revenge for those of us who cannot force ourselves to complete such a feat. We give a "victory" party for participants, a party that appears to be motivated by admiration for the accomplishment of the day. Not a nice restful evening in front of the fire, but a lively, loud dance with a bit of volley ball on the side. Can you guess which guests inevitably last until dawn?

Happy 25 miles a week, Will.
Dee

DOWN TO BASICS

Dear Sis,

When we first moved to Alaska, I remember discussions about how to identify a long time resident. One of the explanations that stuck with me at the time, because I considered it so outlandish was this:

At any gathering of two or more, to segregate sourdough (old timer) from cheechako (new comer), circulate slowly with an attentive ear. Those people intently discussing their septic systems are the real Alaskans.

It's true! Sidle up to the most intense discussion between the loftiest minds and be prepared to hear plenty of technical potty talk.

Waste disposal is a real problem in the frozen north. So often the ground won't accept it. So from my perspective, it isn't at all out of line for me to write a letter to you about what I've been up to, or down to, lately—digging an outhouse hole.

I began the hole last fall, but didn't get very far, because I'm digging in permafrost. By this time of year what little bit of ground that is going to thaw has done so as much as it might and is certain to begin to freeze again any day. So now is the perfect time to attack. While Middle Child and I were bailing out what I hoped was ice that had been thawed, I reminisced about the first hole I ever dug in this area.

At that time, try as I might, with all due force and diligence, I could not get a shovel to go through the foot thick layer of moss, roots, etc., which carpets the forest. In drizzling rain, I trudged 1/2 a mile down the road to the nearest cabin, plaintively explained my frustration, and asked for advice.

Sipping tea, snug by a crackling fire, two men nodded knowingly as I described my problem. They obviously were familiar with the situation and somewhat amused by my plight. When I paused they said simply, "Get an axe." If I had had one at that moment I would have committed mayhem.

Now I know better. A quick, simple way to pierce that lush growth is indeed with an axe. Then you can lift off dense spongy blocks of tundra and transplant them like turf. Once the carpet is gone a shovel does nicely, for awhile. Then thunk—ice. Now you need a match.

Actually, if you have been digging for a long time that is a welcome sound. It means you get to stop for awhile, a week, a month or a year, but if time is pressing in on you this signals a change of attack. One possibility is to build a fire in the hole you've accomplished, place metal over and hope to gain more ground by thawing.

Unfortunately, the ground you gain is usually not under the fire. The walls are more apt to cave in and put out the fire before any deep heat is applied in the desired direction. This way you begin to develop a shallow dip in the terrain rather than a hole. Which is fine if what you set out to dig was a pond for breeding mosquitoes, but not too useful underneath a compact two holer.

Actually digging in permafrost does have some advantages. Last time I dug in soft, cohesive, yielding dirt I got carried away and had to wait for the family to miss me and bring a ladder so that I could climb out.

You think I'm kidding.

Sis

LETTER WRITING EXPLAINED

October 10, 1977

Dear Sis,

Let me see if I can answer some of your questions. You asked me how I manage to write such interesting letters. Well, first of all, it helps to be so far away and to miss you all so much. Then too I don't really feel that I can afford to use the phone to keep in touch. (Yes, we do have phones in Alaska. They don't work very well, but we do have them.)

When I write to you I sit down with a cup of coffee, pen in hand, and try to think of some of the truly unique aspects of our world up here or of how I can tell of some of the disasters in my life in a lighthearted manner. (This is not to imply that living in Alaska is a disaster.)

Let me give you a for-instance, as Dad always says. Imagine the day that Middle Child and I climbed grimy and tired out of the outhouse hole at the end of a day of digging. We drove to an appropriate establishment to shower. We emerged clean and sweet-smelling to find that the car had a flat tire. Cheerfully we removed the tire. Of course, there was no air in the spare and the tire was ruined and it was a holiday and we were miles from an open service station. (Of course.)

With a little bit of thought and positive attitude there is potential for a cheery letter there. Unfortunately, at the time I didn't embrace the situation as excellent writing material. I just kept biting my lip, swearing and trying to think morale boosting thoughts like: It could be below zero, Edith. (It wasn't.) You could be on the way to a job interview or an important appointment. (I wasn't.) I'm happily unemployed.

Actually, I'm not *un*employed, budding free lance writers tend to *feel* unemployed because paychecks are so few and far between.

Well, anyway, back to the delights of disaster. The way I see it, being able to cheerfully face distressing situations is a sign of growth and maturity. (Either that or a sign of premature senility.)

Until recently I used to get upset about little things, like running out of propane in the middle of baking a 12 egg angel food cake. These days I just grin and think positive. With a bit of luck I might win the Bake-Off with an innovative recipe for egg white soup. As the sign at the propane supplier's says: Why worry about tomorrow when we may not make it through today.

Dear me, I got off the track there, back to your questions. How is my ego? How nice of you to ask. People ask me about my children, my parents, my next door neighbor, my dog, my bus and my best friend, but rarely does anyone inquire after the health and welfare of my ego.

It's fine, thank you. On second thought, it is a little too fine. In fact, I'm a bit concerned about it. It is getting out of hand. It seems to have more courage than I do. I think I may even prefer my old, beaten down mousey original. It never strode off boldly

46

without consulting me or embarked on new projects that I'm not sure I'm quite ready for.

How's my ego, Sis? A bit too sassy these days. How's yours?

me

WAFFLE STOMPER LAMENT

October 17, 1977

Dear Janet,

Do you remember when we were kids how our "new" shoes were the ones that we considered special, no matter how old or shabby they might be.

Guess I haven't changed a whole lot in the last few decades. It just came as quite a shock to me that my waffle stompers have about had it.

Do you call them waffle stompers down there? You know, the sturdy boots with thick black soles that pick up and drop off intricate patterns of mud and snow on clean linoleum.

Mine were good looking as boots go: foreign made, expensive and even a bit fashionable in a rustic sort of way. They felt so good. They fit so fine. They were the most comfortable foot gear I've ever owned. When we bought them, eons ago in Colorado, I expected them to last forever, but I hadn't bargained on how essential to existence they are in Alaska.

Mine were light enough for running, biking, canoeing, berry picking and back packing; heavy enough to help thrust shovel into dirt or snow and provide protection from chain saw, axe and drawknife. They served as cross-country ski boots, boat boots, early winter boots, mud boots and break-up boots (with a bit of water proofing). Up here you need warm boots for running on the beach.

Many's the time they complimented my plaid wool pants suit at the nippy turn of the season, and when it was super icy and slick I've been known to wear them to a concert or play underneath a long flowing skirt. (Hope my mother never finds out about that.)

The only thing I haven't done is sleep in them and I won't swear to that.

Throughout the years they have carried me over countless miles of tundra and turf. Like loyal friends they have provided firm support, worked hard with me, stood by me in times of trouble, jumped for joy with me, and adjusted well to my peculiar patterns such as the way I walk and the hours I keep.

It's sad to see them looking worn, disappointing to realize that they actually leak and can't be mended. My "new" shoes are getting old. I guess even boots deserve to retire after a job well done.

I cannot begin to compute a cost per mile equivalent, however, my calculator indicates that they have served me well, with no maintenance whatsoever, for approximately $3.58 a year. For less than a penny a day I have had faultless service! Transportation like that is hard to beat.

Time marches on. The baby who sat on my hip when I first weighed the wisdom of spending so much money on foot gear accompanied me today when I shopped for replacements. He was barefoot then. Today we bought him a pair of boots two sizes larger than mine.

If my *"new"* boots last half as long as the original pair I could be a grandmother before I need to replace them.

What a thought!

> Write when you get a chance,
> Dee

THE SEASON'S OVER!

October 24, 1977

Dear Judy, Buck, Aaron and Sarah,

How are you enjoying California?

I thought of you in your wanderings when I first noticed that the tourists up here are all gone. I was driving into town and suddenly missed the out-of-staters. I began watching license plates carefully to confirm my suspicion. I almost ran a stop light and got buzzed by a low flying Camaro, but sure enough. All the licenses were Alaskan.

In seasons past, I have dismissed the tourists as necessary nuisances that crowded our parking lots and slowed down the traffic. This is the first year I've really appreciated and enjoyed our visitors. I suspect this change in my attitude came about because of personal contact with some of the travelers. (Working in a motel has hidden fringe benefits.)

The questions were fun. "How long have you *been* here?" "Oh! You mean you *live* here?" "Do you *like* it?" "Are you an *Alaskan?*" "Do you *ever* get used to the daylight at night?" "How do you survive the winter cold?" "What do you *do* up here?" "If you only had one day to spend in your town how would you spend it?" (The answers I got to that question when I tried it on some of the locals were *very* interesting.) "What does sixty below zero feel like?" And so forth.

The travelers' experiences are enviable: Glacier Bay to Prudhoe Bay; Dawson to Little Diomede; the Aleutians; Southeastern; the Brooks Range and the Bering Sea. How I would like to see those places.

Their enthusiasm was delightful and chided me for my casual attitude toward the wonderment that is Alaska. "It is so vast!" "So magnificent!" "Inexpressibly beautiful!" "Inspiring." "Truly a fascinating place."

Their histories were charming. "We discussed a trip like this on our first date. That was 32 years ago." "Everyone back home thinks we're foolish to be spending so much money and driving so far, but we just had to find out what Alaska is all about." "I invested in a piece of that pipeline and decided to come up and take a look at it." "This trip means we'll have been in all but two states, and we'll visit those two on the way back home."

I guess the reason I noticed their absence this year is that I enjoyed their presence.

One evening I overheard some New Yorkers say to a very special friend of mine, "Nancy, our trip to Alaska has been made much more memorable for having met you."

That was it exactly! Summer was much more interesting and more fun for having contact with those individuals that we usually lump into the category of "tourist." I discovered that underneath their label they are just people with whom I have a lot in common. We like to travel, we are impressed with Alaska and we enjoy other people.

The tourists, the geese and the summer have left us for awhile, but they will be back. Theirs is a round trip. So, in spite of the snow on the ground, we can safely say—Summer is on its way.

> Hurry Home,
> Edee

TRICK OR TREAT

October 31, 1977

Dear Don,

Remember that day in October so many years ago, when our 3rd grader, a veteran Alaskan of two months, came home disgusted and out of sorts? It seems her class had just established a pen pal relationship with a class somewhere else in America and she was thoroughly disgusted.

"Honestly!" She exclaimed. "They ask such *dumb* questions. Do we have Halloween? Do we speak English? What kind of clothes do we wear?" (Bulky and expensive, I remember suggesting.) "Do we live in an igloo?" (That apartment did tend to collect ice on the inner walls and at times we thought a nice snug igloo might be warmer.)

The turn-about came at teacher conference time when I discovered our little died-in-the-wool Alaskan's impatience with ignorance was causing an in-house problem.

Our one time "model" student was labeled as "disruptive," "unwilling to respect the rights of others," etc.

How distressing! When I exhibited mild hysteria concerning this, the teacher tried to calm me. The problem, it seemed, was that our "veteran Alaskan" was too wise in the ways of the

50

world and far too outspoken about "foreign" things such as elevators, freeway cloverleafs and places on the map like Disneyland and Denver, Colorado. She tended to become quite impatient with her uninformed classmates and to loudly and without waiting her turn enlighten them.

"Her enthusiasm is admirable." The teacher assured me. "Her knowledge and experience are a welcome contribution, but her outbursts are disruptive."

I was apologetic, but relieved. We certainly didn't want the children to grow up with no knowledge of the world beyond. Courteous, yes; unaware, no.

A few years later, we were discussing a trip *out* to celebrate Christmas with grandparents.

"Wait until you see the huge airports outside!" Big Sister bragged. For we had discovered that Middle Child could not remember much of the world she had left behind.

"We have a nice big airport here." She pouted loyally.

"You, Baby!" Big Sister insisted. "The cities, the highways, the buildings, *everything* everywhere else in much different than here and much, much bigger. Wait and see."

I remember it well. Taking off on the Red Eye Special. (For some reason the one direct flight out of here was at 1 a.m. and affectionately called the Red Eye Special.) We landed in Seattle in the middle of the night and as I herded three sleepy and excited children down an interminable "ramp" to catch the next plane, I tugged, and shoved, and scolded. I lost sight of the significance of the event for the little people until. . . .

A small girl gasped in amazement. I stopped and quickly turned around. There stood Middle Child with her face pressed against the dark window-wall staring out in wonder at all she ever saw of Seattle—a multi-story parking garage dotted with cars.

"OH!" She whispered, in a tone of awe. "You are right, Lia. This city is much bigger than Fairbanks!"

Those were the days.

Fondly,
Edee

HAMMER FASTER

Dear Sharron and Will,

Congratulations on the purchase of your new home! ! ! ! It sounds huge! I realize you will be terribly busy, but do tell me more about it, please, soon, soon, soon.

Realizing you two have bought a big, old "new" house which undoubtedly is even finished set me to thinking yet again about housing up here.

I was driving home really late one night believing that everyone but me was asleep when a house with light blazing from every opening came into view. I was tempted to stop and join them for I knew from experience what was going on inside. The lights would not be from a wild party or a family of insomniacs. In process was bound to be a wee hour assault upon an unheatable house.

In the middle of the largest room there would be a space heater roaring. A space heater looks like a glowing cannon and in such situations it issues forth great quantities of noise, fire and smell, but very little heat.

How can heat be contained when the visqueen hanging over the holes that will eventually hold windows and doors keeps flapping in the breeze? Breeze? No, we've actually very little wind up here. The visqueen pulsates to accompany the whoosh of the space heater. It is quite a sympathetic interaction, if you think about it, but probably lost on the people within.

The builders are crouched in various positions with a mittened hand holding a hammer and a gloved hand holding a nail. They wiggle their toes and shiver in time to the beat of their pounding, sweating underneath a heavy jacket and coveralls. Cold and sweaty, a truly Alaskan experience.

To appreciate this you must realize that it is already very cold up here and the world is covered with snow. Elsewhere this particular structure might be inhabitable. The roof is on, thank goodness, the siding is up, etc. However, as October comes to a close, unheatable is unliveable in Fairbanks.

How well I remember that year long ago. Friends gathered to

help us get into the barn-like structure and "Get those children out of the tent and under a roof." We appreciated the assistance, but what a cold roof! The furnace was not in the basement as we had planned, but "somewhere" between here and Seattle. We painted the floor and it was so cold that the paint wouldn't dry. So *in* the house we were indeed, huddled cold and forlorn in one small corner gazing out at a great sea of wet paint.

As I was driving by the busy builders' house that night, I had been envying you your move and deploring my own very unfinished home, but somehow when I reached my door the sheetrock on the walls gave me comfort instead of a nagging reminder that spackling, taping, sanding and painting are yet to come. The unsightly ceiling of sagging vapor barrier and insulation seemed suddenly snug and secure and the trimless windows caused me to think, how nice to have glass, as well as, plastic in that hole in the wall. All things are relative.

Do you have a picture of your house that you could send us? I have too much to do here to come down this winter.

Congratulations!
Dee

WHAT'S IN A WORD?

November 14, 1977

Dear Chris, Tom, Cindy and Jennifer,

Hey! You are right. I cannot find that word in my dictionary either, even in my unabridged.

Sorry for using a word that means nothing to you, but it sure was fun to get your ideas on what that stuff might be.

No, Tom, it isn't fertilizer, but it is true that we use it on our gardens.

Cindy was correct. It covers the walls in Jill's room and in the hall, but it is definitely not wallpaper or paneling. (How I wish it were.)

Tell your neighbor it isn't wax. When I said we cover the motorcycles and bicycles with it to protect them from the weather I mean we toss it over them, not rub it on them.

Took me awhile to figure out why Jennifer thought it was glass cleaner, until I realized that I must have mentioned putting it over the windows inside and out.

Chris, you were close with your speculation of material. We have indeed used it to make a tent, and for make-shift rain gear. We know of others who have used it for crib sheets, table cloths and slippery sleds.

When I called building supply stores to find out another name for it I found out that it is made out of polyethylene; that it comes 2, 4, 6 and 10 mils thick, as large as 40' x 100' and black as well as clear. No one, however, could tell me why we call it what we do.

One man speculated that our word was originally a brand name of a material which was first used to package hot dogs. Everyone kindly checked and found that this word appears no where on any of the boxes or in any of the catalogues now available.

Basically we use it to keep cold air out, warm air in and moisture on one side or the other. One family covered the crawl space under their house with it and when the interior gets too dry they pull back a corner to let a little dampness in. Stephen lined a plywood box with it. After hauling fish and ice 600 miles he determined that it does not do much to control the flow of smell.

Vapor barrier, humidifier, tarp, cold catcher, heat holder, rain shelter, all that and more, but yesterday I discovered a brand new use for it: newcomer identifier.

In my search for the origin of the word, I called a reference librarian at the University and asked if he would look up the word for me in the most recent, complete and appropriate dictionary.

His response was, "What's 'visqueen'?"

"New to Alaska?" I asked.

"Yes." He replied.

"Well, though I'm not sure why, 'visqueen' is what we call

the polyethylene sheeting that we use to. . ." And before I knew it I was the one supplying the definition.

Shall be more careful with my vocabulary in the future.

Keep in touch,
Dee

TO BE OR NOT TO BE?

November 21, 1977

Dear Sis,

Are you asking me to talk you into or out of becoming a cocktail waitress? I'll tell you a little bit about my experience up here and let you decide for yourself.

For me the drastic difference between my cloistered, basic world in the woods and the nightlife in our boom town was one of the most fantastic things about the job. (I suspect you might not find that contrast in suburban Sacramento.) To put down a chain saw, shovel or hammer; take off my grubbies; slip on a slinky jersy jumpsuit and glide into a candle lit lounge was half the fun. Sort of like playing Cinderella.

It boggled my mind each time I cashed out a customer's tab and saw that the cost of the evening's drinks exceeded my weekly income. I remember one fellow flipping through a deck of un-cashed paychecks for the oldest one because: "The company gets huffy if I don't use 'em soon enough."

When I first took the job I was apprehensive. "What if there's trouble?" I asked.

"Oh, just refer any problems to the bartender." Said my prospective employer.

That calmed my fears, until I met the bartender. She was half my size, mildmannered and soft spoken. Sort of like having a kitten for a watch dog.

I needn't have worried. The establishment was very respectable, the clientele congenial and polite. Although we did have a few friendly regulars who chased around the room on hands and knees threatening to bite me on the ankle, they never tried hard enough to catch me.

It's a little bit like giving a party every night. You make sure the guests glasses are full and they're having a nice time. You get left with the dishes and the mess, but at least in this case someone else foots the bill for the refreshments.

If your morale needs a boost—do it! As the evening progresses you get prettier. Though the compliments do tend to get less understandable. I don't think it's legal to send through the mail some of the comments and conversations, but believe me, it doesn't take long to learn which leers to lend an ear to and which to ignore. (I must admit, the only one who ever said to me, "What's a nice girl like you doing in a place like this" was me.)

I did have some trouble with my responsibilities. My social worker side kept coming out and I'd catch myself saying, "Oh, you aren't ready for another one *yet.*" (That is frowned upon in the business.)

Since the most difficult thing for me to do each day is get out of bed, the evening hours suited me perfectly. Also I liked the idea that my midday maximum production time belonged to me and my employer got the energy that was left over at the end of the day.

If you do take a job down there, write and tell me all about it. Up here we have traditions such as "six-packing" and "timbering the bar." I wonder if they are unique to Alaska? I'd like to know just how different we really are.

Promise me! ! ! ! Whatever you decide to do, don't you dare tell Mom I encouraged you.

Good luck in decision making,
Sis

Oh! P. S. A "six-pack" is just that. Someone orders you six of whatever you're drinking and the rules go "drink 'em or wear 'em." Makes things a bit rowdy at times because the only appropriate retort is to answer in kind.

"Timbering the bar" is buying drinks for the house. In some establishments this occurs automatically when one foolishly or intentionally rings a bell that is prominently placed.

NORTH OF THE BORDER

November 28, 1977

Dear Jay,

No, sorry, there is no way I can visit Mexico this winter. (Though I surely would like to do so.) When the first blast of sub-zero weather hits here each year I always claim that Alaska is the true Land of Mañana.

My car is calibrated. It starts, but with increasing difficulty, as the temperature slides toward zero. At precisely zero and any point below it insists upon being plugged in. Now I know this. I could prepare for it. During the crisp fall weather I could set out the timer, extension cord, battery warmer, hood blanket, and other appropriate paraphernalia. Do I?

Of course, I do. The day after the car freezes solid and causes me to be late to work.

I've known since July that the puppy chewed the weather stripping off the front door. However, it wasn't until there was a visible cloud of icy air whistling through the gap that I swung into action.

Picture me suited up in full winter gear, sitting on the frozen porch with the door wide open, painfully hammering carpeting along the bottom of the door. Just think of all the mosquitoes I avoided by doing that chore at sub-zero temperatures.

All spring, summer and fall I have tripped over brush and thought "good kindling," noticed down trees and registered, "ought to cut that up," nagged myself with "Edith, you really do need to start gathering firewood." Last week I burned the last log, twig and Sunday Times and began eyeing a pile of 2 x 4's. When I realized with astonishment that I was contemplating which pieces of furniture we could do without, I finally took up shovel and saw and trudged off into the woods. Scarved up to my eye brows, I stumbled around searching for "solid fuel." It's simply too hot to think about fires in the summer.

Of course, I'm going to re-visqueen (remember visqueen?) the windows, but I hate to lose the view as long as there is some light to each day. That plastic is not exactly crystal clear.

In late December I'll be complaining about the trials of wielding a stapler in the dark and the impact of cold on plastic. Meanwhile I'm busy knitting mittens that it is now too cold to wear.

Our floor is terribly cold. There is insulation hanging down and some completely missing underneath the house. Last summer each time I thought about this chore the canoe, the garden or the sun beckoned and mosquitoes encouraged me to delay slithering under there to lie on my back and knock fiberglass into my eyes.

With the cold came the realization that when the days are warm and buggy it must be cool under the house. I think I'll do that job next summer covered with "Cutters" rather than next week bundled in down. We don't spend much time on the floor anyway.

This winter, instead of lying on the beach I'll huddle by the fire and when the children exclaim, "Mom! There is *ice* on that wall." I'll nod and answer firmly, "Yes, I know. I'm going to chink those logs—tomorrow."

Oh, Jay, if you do come north this year, the first week or so in May is fine. You can help me remove my studded snow tires. (They're illegal after April 30.)

Adios,
Edee

COAL? SHE SAID

December 5, 1977

Dear Sis,

What can I say?

The first deep dip of the thermometer always takes me and my vehicle down with it so rather than write about this week while the wounds are still fresh I thought I'd send you a portrayal of a near actual conversation from days gone by.

"Coal?" She said. "You have got to be kidding!"

"Coal!" He said. "I am serious."

"Don't be silly. Coal is what people heated with in the olden days."

"When I was growing up in Pennsylvania, we heated with coal and that was not in the olden days."

"When I was growing up we used electricity, like civilized people. We are not going to burn black rocks like primitives. We will burn wood."

"This wood won't burn."

"That's silly, wood always burns. Why my Daddy. . ."

"Your Daddy uses two-year seasoned oak. Your Daddy lives in California. You live in interior Alaska where there is no such thing as oak. In fact, right now there is damned little wood in town."

"Well, there are certainly plenty of trees."

"Those trees are spindly spruce which require hundreds of years to grow and a couple of minutes to burn, aspen which are brilliant with fall color, but useless for heat, and birch which. . ."

"You're not going to cut the birch! Those are the only decent trees around!"

"Precisely."

"Precisely?"

"We live in a very *cold* climate. The same cold climate that demands we maintain auxiliary heat due to frequent power outages causes our trees to be less than ideal for heating."

"But the oil?"

"The oil furnace depends upon electricity."

"Oh." Pause. "Of course."

"Remember, the last time the electricity went out you lost all your house plants, the pipes burst, and we damned near froze. Now we have this $400.00 solid fuel burning stove to combat that problem. In view of the fact that there is no wood available to burn in this decorative, but useful investment, I think we need to consider alternatives."

"Alternatives?" She said.

"Coal." He said.

And indeed, they did burn coal that year.

However, I still prefer wood.

Catch you later. I've got to go out and check the battery charger.

Much love,
Sis

PLEASE FIX IT

December 12, 1977

Dear Someone Who Cares,

I drove past one of those time and temperature signs on my way home this evening and it registered -37 degrees. That really made my day. Of course, I would have been happier if it had read -47 degrees, but -37 degrees was quite satisfactory.

I wriggled my toes frantically to try to divert the pain and encourage circulation as I contemplated the temperature. It felt good to see those numbers. I like having the thermometer say very cold when I'm feeling very cold.

I was, of course, in the car with the heat on, I think. I'm sure I was in the car and I'm sure I had the heater switched on, but the car's and my circulating systems have a lot in common. Something hot runs around the hoses inside both of us, but it doesn't really warm up anything so as you'd notice it.

Anyway, discomfort aside, this is my winter to see -67° and I'm anxious to get on with it. I've never really believed in -67°. The first winter we were up here it was sixty below a lot, or at least too much. That year some of the places a bit south of here claimed readings of -70° and beyond, but I've never really seen anything colder than -65° myself.

This winter I'm in luck. I've arranged to spend a certain amount of time driving through and working in the cold pockets of the area.

However, I have a problem. I depend upon those lighted up messages in the sky things. We are very sophisticated up here when it comes to lights in the sky, both natural and contrived.

We have a sign that does everything but take phone messages. (Wouldn't it be nice to be driving home and see, "Mom, I'm at Peter's. I'll be late for dinner.") I could shop leisurely for a change.

Anyway, those ingenious electronic devises are useful, decorative, entertaining, uplifting, educational and reassuring. I've arranged my 36 mile drive to and from work so that I pass at least three as I travel. That way I can tell that I am on time, where I am (in times of ice fog, you can use all the clues you can get) and whether I'm getting colder or warmer. That latter is important to me. I hate to be misled by the discomfort of my skin or my extremities into believing that I am suffering more than I really am.

Well, anyway, the problem is, one of these splendid message boards doesn't work. Each time I drive past and it tells me that I am early (which is incorrect) and then refuses to tell me the temperature, I get furious. What pleasure is there in braving the elements for an hour as you strike out into the darkness if there is no printed verification of your accomplishment?

To make matters worse, the one of those thingies that doesn't work is the one that is going to register -67°. So please won't someone who knows how, fix that beacon so that the belows beam from above. The sooner the better or we'll never know when we have hit 67 below.

In advance, I thank you for brightening up my day.

        Sincerely,
        Edith C. Rohde

IT'S ALMOST WINTER

December 19, 1977

Dear Mom and Dad,

This week we celebrate the first day of winter and witness the shortest day of the year.

We're ready though. We've been having a full-scale dress rehearsal of both events for a couple of weeks now.

We've practiced important things like minus fifty degrees, severe ice fog, cars that won't function, frozen pipes and various other appropriate exercises. I feel relatively certain that we are just about ready to jump right into the season with a fair amount of skill, resignation and appreciation.

"Appreciation?" You exclaim. "She's got to be kidding! What's to appreciate about conditions like that?"

Well, believe me, at fifty below, one truly appreciates the simple things in life, the little joys that contribute satisfaction to daily existence such as:

—an extension cord that never falls out of a parking lot outlet, (You cannot imagine this until you've seen an entire parking lot full of ordinary cars plugged into poles with the fervent hope that they will function in spite of the cold as a result of the constant injection of electricity.)

—the sign of an idiot light glowing with electricity on a frosty bumper after a hard day at the office,

—the vroom, vroom, vroom of an engine that belongs to your car and starts!!

—the realization that you really are where you'd hoped you might be in spite of the ice fog and the fact that you thought you had four more blocks to go,

—indoor plumbing,

—indoor plumbing that hasn't frozen.

In a climate like this we live a simple life. The population tends not to think in terms of grandeur, great wealth or glory, but to hope for basic, realistic, though perhaps impossible dreams such as:

—a car heater that heats the driver in addition to a pie-shaped clearing on the windshield,

—foot and hand gear that actually keep the old hoofs and paws pain-free,

—a chance to see the sky,

—an announcement that due to lack of appreciation and proper respect all severe negative temperatures have been cancelled.

Usually at this time of year I am pushing the idea that our day ought to include a long early lunch followed by a siesta break. This is not so we can snooze, but so we can go outdoors, face the south and bask in the sight of the sun while it is so briefly with us.

During the last few weeks I've decided that we are actually better off spending as much time as possible in a clean well-lit building and pretending that there is no out of doors. It is possible that the sun has been cancelled due to heavy ice fog. Maybe we won't have a shortest day this year.

On to cheerier thoughts. You asked what I ʋanted for Christmas. All I really want is 20 degrees, and I'm very flexible about that. I'd prefer 20 above and plenty of lovely, fresh skiable snow, but if that's not possible I'll take 20° warmer than what we've been having.

Just send warm wishes and we'll be happy.

Love,
Dee

SURF AND SAND

December 27, 1977

Dear Buck, Judy, Aaron and Sarah,

Hawaii for Christmas! ! ! ?

You have got to be kidding.

How can a fine, traditional Alaskan family like yours be celebrating Christmas in Hawaii?

Don't you feel absolutely un-American?

Can you really find satisfaction in sorting sea shells instead of stringing cranberries and popcorn?

When our local school Christmas concerts were being cancelled due to heavy ice fog and fifty below, I found it hard to believe that you were winging your way from sunny California to the sandy beaches of a land where the sun shines all day long instead of just at noon.

What was it like?

Did you decorate a palm tree?

Was there a chimney in the condominium for Santa to squeeze into?

What kind of Christmas stockings did you hang up if you were wearing sandals or going barefoot?

Try as I might I cannot fathom you basking in the sun as I shovel snow.

Last week I was standing in a long check-out line juggling purchases, purse, mittens, hat, scarf and parka. As I stared out at the dark, exhaust-clouded parking lot, it wasn't easy to imagine you four swimsuit clad, encumbered only by suntan oil, scrunching your toes into warm white sand and gazing out at the pounding surf.

Gracious how we miss you.

Did you miss skiing over in the sunset after Christmas breakfast to thank the neighbors for their exquisite handmade gifts?

Or sharing your holiday with newcomers to the cold country so they don't feel so far from home?

Did you think about the sauna after supper, about rolling in the snow and sledding by lantern light? Or lying on the rya rug in front of the fire and wondering how the kids can crack one more pistachio nut after such a splendid meal?

Can the salty sea spray of surfing, skin diving and snorkeling really replace wet snow flakes on eye lashes and cheeks? Somehow a luau and leis just doesn't seem suitable at holiday time.

Well, I won't knock it since I haven't tried it. After all, considering how many of you "true" Alaskans are over there right now, surf-sand-and-sunshine could become the new "traditional" Alaskan holiday fare.

Merry Christmas, Happy New Year and Aloha with a twinge of envy. Hurry back home again to shiver properly with the rest of us.

Edee

GETTIN' STRAIGHT IN '78

January 3, 1978

Dear Sharron and Will,

You would be proud of me. One entire category of my extensive list of New Year's Resolutions focuses on physical exercise. You know, like cold showers, team sports and good clean living. I resolved to:

—swim every Tuesday and Thursday morning,

—play volleyball every Wednesday afternoon,

—ski each weekend,

—and go dancing as often as possible.

I didn't exactly *accidently* hit upon this athletic emphasis. As winter progresses my physical activity dwindles down to eating, sleeping and sweeping. Just about drastic dark time I begin to feel, look and act like a well-fed animal going into hibernation. So I want to stir up the vital juices, liven up my life and slim down my waist.

My other resolutions were less vigorous:

—rush out to begin Christmas shopping the minute the first snow falls (which is usually in September anyway),

—scurry around to get those presents mailed by Halloween,

—face the fact that I personally was meant to send out Valentines rather than Christmas cards,

—write home more often,

—avoid writing home when suffering from the winter blues and blahs,

—arrange my life so that I don't get the winter blues and blahs too often. This would insure more time available to write home.

Actually, my first a "four" mentioned resolutions will help combat the dark days double "b's," but just in case that isn't enough, I made some resolutions that fall into a local category:

—never idle my car, (There is the possibility that the carbon monoxide is poisoning our minds and causing us to be grouchy with ice fog.)

—cease envying those who winter in Mexico,

—plan a trip to someplace in this vast and glorious state that I have not yet visited,

—each and every day appreciate what a magnificent, fantastic, beautiful world we live in. Watch the sun causing the Alaska Range to blush, ponder the shapes of the snow-clad trees, examine a snow flake resting on a mitten, marvel at the dance of the aurora borealis.

Oh dear. I'm running out of time and space, but I'm not running out of resolutions. It's a good thing that there is an entire year in which to carry them out.

There are lots and lots more, but the one that is most important to all of us up here is:

—keep in close touch with good people.

Happy 1978 to two of the best people I know!

Miss you much,
Dee

WE'RE GAINING!

January 9, 1978

Dear Mom and Dad,

You are right. The darkness bothers me. I tell you it doesn't. I tell me it doesn't. I pretend it doesn't, but it does. I ought to ask some other people how they feel about it, but I work so hard at trying to convince myself I don't care that to discuss it would be self-defeating.

The question might seem a bit silly, too. "Excuse me, Sir, how do you feel about winter darkness?" Like asking how one feels about breathing. What alternative do we have?

Winter weather comes and goes. There is an element of uncertainty. There is variety. Weather can be cold and get colder. It can suddenly skyrocket to above zero. It can plummet to belows you wouldn't believe. There might be snow, clouds, the threat of rain, lovely clear skies, a bit of breeze. It changes. I like that.

Toward darkness, however, we trudge ever onward. No turning back, no respite, the minutes drop off: 10, 9, 8, 7, 6 . . . down we go to 3 hours and 42 minutes.

Three hours and forty two minutes of almost light. The amount of light you actually see depends. It depends upon what side of the street you live on. How many trees are nearby. Whether or not there are clouds. How cold it is, and your ability to remember to look in exactly the right direction at precisely the appropriate moment.

You down there need to know that when the sun does appear it travels across the horizon to the south, just like this ". . . . .," and for about that long. If there is a tall building "BUILDING" between you and ". . . . .," a good portion of the "light" of the day never reaches you.

I have driven up out of a dark gully after spending the afternoon with a friend to discover that those lucky people who live on the other side of the hill are having daytime. Fancy that!

I know you worry about my mental health. (It's no secret that you think I'm crazy for living here.) However, I want to reassure you that the darkness isn't really all that bad.

There are all sorts of advantages to it. Most of which have slipped my mind at the moment. At any rate—"don't worry 'bout me." We are presently climbing up out of the depths of darkness at a remarkable rate. By the time you receive this letter we will have gained almost one full hour of daylight for a grand, glorious total of 4 hours and 36 minutes.

By Valentines Day we practically live like people with a fantastic 8 hours and 25 minutes of basically real visible sunshine. The glowing orb moves toward its "proper" place in the sky and we inch toward the phenomenon that makes it all worth while—the perpetual daylight that we tend to forget we are grudgingly purchasing on time, with due interest, throughout the dreary winter.

And so "as the sun sets slowly in the south," I bid you fond adieu, at 2:02. Brighter days are on their way.

Love you much,
Dee

SHORTLY HOWEVER

January 16, 1978

Dear Chris, Tom, Cindy and Jennifer,

The children were aghast when they received your letter.

"You mean they don't have Short Courses in the Lower 48!?!?" They exclaimed in disbelief. "What do they *do*?"

Certainly you must have an equivalent. Our Short Courses are non-credit classes of various types that are self-supporting, but coordinated through the community college. They are super!

The kids have been involved in them since we first arrived in Alaska. The classes were originally under the auspices of the University. Consequently, Young Son's first certificate for completion of a "University" class was received before he was five years old.

How well I remember the hours spent sitting in the bleachers with another mother. We knit mittens, chatted and winced as our wee ones bobbed about in the water. The swimming teacher was a struggling University of Alaska swim team member, but to the children he was King Neptune. I do believe they would have tried to fly if he had suggested it.

Many people must share the philosophy that once you have children toilet trained it's time to get them waterproofed. For the swimming classes have always been a major part of the Short Course program.

The classes are not just for kids, however. There is literally something for everyone offered each season. There is even kindergarten for puppies.

The catalogue is worth having for its entertainment value. The art work is always good, the course descriptions well-written and some of the course titles inevitably rate a chuckle.

This session there is Macramania; Diaper Gym; What's Going On In There?; The Portable Lunch; and Introduction to Mud and. . . . I wonder whatever happended to last fall's So You Want to Be a Star and Find Us in the Museum.

Another enjoyable aspect of the catalogue is keeping track of the instructors. It reads like Who's-Who-and-up-to-what-in-the-community this season. You learn which mother is feeling so confident that she is willing to teach How to Deal with Your Teenager, and which recent student has discovered that now he or she can teach what was just learned.

With a slight stretch of the imagination, the arrangement is reminiscent of ancient education. The wise, the talented, the enthusiastic, mingle and share with the uninitiated. Thus knowledge, crafts and appreciation are spread throughout the tribe.

The catalogue always boosts my morale when I realize that in our remote community, just ordinary people can sign up to experience kayaking, calligraphy, tipi living, Russian and Ukranian egg decorating, judo, belly dancing, hand writing analysis, yoga, curling, karate, Swedish massage, laying linoleum, trapping, fantasy war game construction, snorkeling, and dowsing—the art of divining and its many uses.

On second thought, I agree with the kids. If you don't have Short Courses down there what *do* you do?

Until next time,
Dee

LIGHT'S OUT

January 23, 1978

Dear Buck, Judy, Aaron and Sarah,

Guess what. We haven't had a good, snuggle up to the fire, ghost story telling, popcorn popping power outage yet this winter. I really miss those.

How can we appreciate doing without running water if the lights don't go out? How can we relax in the glow of flickering candles, snug and secure that the pipes we don't have won't freeze if the heat doesn't go off all over town?

Where is the one winter-time justification for emptying a slop bucket if there is no call to listen sympathetically when the fluent among us relate horror tales of thawing and pumping?

That line of reasoning might seem narrow and selfish, but actually it represents a great deal of concern for the community. Power outages are traditional. They are inevitable, like snow, sub-zero, ice fog and noontime sunsets, all aspects of life of which we can be proud.

To do without power outages could cause widespread uncertainty and insecurity. We might begin to question our ruggedness, to suspect we cannot brave the elements or survive the rigors of life in the frozen north.

Think of all the power outages you have experienced. (Not counting the New Year's Eve that someone flipped the circuit breaker.) Such meaningful memories! What a shame it would be to see this aspect of the charm, the adventure and the challenge of living in our pioneer town eliminated—another victim of civilization and increased technology.

Oh, I'll admit that some of my security comes from finally having wood heat as well as oil and electricity. I do not deny the six month mourning period that year I suffered the loss of all 32 of my house plants, not to mention the fact that the children got pretty cold and frightened.

Nevertheless, I do miss the excitement, the eerieness of sudden darkness, the helplessness, the futility of resisting and consequent relaxation. (Though since we cook with propane I suppose I could bake cookies or bread, by candlelight.)

I miss the phone calls, the visits from nearby neighbors who never have time or reason to call otherwise. Some great friendships have grown out of the simple question, "Is your electricity off too?"

One of my favorite powerless experiences occurred when I was working as a cocktail waitress. In the already dim lit lounge, we lost what little light we ever used, and also use of the blender and the mix dispenser. Everyone had to be satisfied with rocks

or water. Satisfied they were, for customers became quite friendly and "round" after "round" was bought for the house. The
help could hardly keep up with the generosity.

Watching the congeniality created by this adversity was
fascinating. So was the fact, lost on most, that since it was 11
p.m. in the middle of June they had only to step out the door to
shed a little light on the situation.

Come to think of it, our blackouts are probably one of the
few things we have in common with New York City. Given that
bit of wisdom, I'll have to reconsider my conviction that they
foster our pioneer spirit.

Meanwhile, how is New Zealand?

Edee

WOOD IS WARMER

January 30, 1978

Dear Mom and Dad,

Having just tended the fire it is time to tend to letter writing.
We have had a whole week now of above zero temperatures!
Such a blessing at this time of year.

This means that in spite of the fact that the puppy chewed the
weather stripping off the door again there is no wind blowing in,
no ice on the inside of the door and no pronounced draft across
the floor. Of course, there is also no chance I'll remember to
replace the weather stripping until some of those conditions do
reoccur.

I know what you are thinking, Dad. No, there is also no
chance we'll get rid of the dog. That animal worships Middle
Child and there are far too few advantages to being middle child
as it is.

Back to the issue of heating with wood. While it doesn't sur-
prise me at all that in this age of advanced technology, *I* heat
with wood, I am amazed at how many other people up here do
so too.

What is the allure? Economy? I'm not so sure. There may be some people with ready access to "solid fuel," but for most of us once we have cleared a spot for building the house and planting the garden we don't exactly end up with a lifetime supply of firewood.

Wood is called the conservationist's fuel, but I have great difficulty accepting the idea that in short order we can turn into ashes what Mother Nature took so long to nurture. In fact, my land is a disaster area of leaning, struggling trees which I will not take an axe or saw to because it pains me to hurt a living tree. Would you believe all my wood gathering had been of downed wood? That's all my conscience will allow.

I've been told that if I cut down the scraggly ones the others will flourish, but who am I to decide who should live and who should die? I was pretty scraggly too in my younger days.

Someone told me that even if you buy wood it is cheaper heat than oil or electricity, but with gathering, hauling, cutting, splitting, stacking and tending the fire who had the time to stop and do a price comparison?

With hesitation, I insist that wood heat is warmer. I don't want to defend that statement, but in our house it feels that way and I do believe it. How else could I convince myself to put up with the mess and bother?

I might claim to prefer wood due to the aesthetics of dancing flames and glowing coals, but of course the big black monster in the corner is kept shut tight most of the time. I do prefer the snap, crackle and pop of a fire to the drone of a furnace.

In all honesty, it isn't even relevant that the Scandinavian Stump Eater requires no servicing and creates no repair bills. What it boils down to is that building and tending a fire is simply more satisfying and challenging than flipping a switch.

I must admit that I'm hooked. I, who would rather sleep than eat or do almost anything else, will get up in the middle of the night to put a log on rather than allow the furnace to warm us as we sleep. *That* you can see is the true reason I'm extra glad it's above 0° these days.

Keep Warm,
Dee

"TO A TRAVELER"
OR "HEY, YOU DOWN THERE"

February 6, 1978

Dear Kathy,

Where are you? I can't forward your mail because by the time your itinerary reaches me you have already gotten to the part that reads: "after that I'm not sure."

Cheerful and helpful though our post office people are they say "probably headed south" won't do as a forwarding address.

Have you forgotten home so quickly? Remember this is Alaskan mail service, not the pony express. It takes a great deal of time for your letters to find their way up here.

Try this: Imagine someone in a South Dakota post office, your handsomely addressed envelope in hand, looking up to say, "A-L-A-S-K-A, do we have a basket for letters to that country?"

"Country!?" says the person at his elbow. "AL-ask-A isn't a country, it is a territory where they had a gold rush once. It is called Eureka now and it's in California."

"No! No! Wait." Interrupts a well-informed eaves-dropper. (If you and I are lucky.) "Alaska still exists. It's a land in the north where there are wolves, igloos and brilliant lights in the sky. Oh, wait a minute. This letter only has regular postage on it, we can't send a letter so far away with regular postage. Hmmmmmmmm. Oh, let's send it anyway. Those people up there are isolated, out of touch with the rest of the world. Here, I'll take it. It goes in the bag marked foreign ports."

Once the letter does find its way to Fairbanks it still has to come across town and you know how long *that* takes.

Then imagine me receiving a letter from you, racing home, writing a quick reply, checking the calendar, running my finger down your list of addresses to the appropriate date and reading, "send you more details soon." Soon isn't soon enough!

As I was saying, where are you?

I wanted you to call collect because I hate to break this to you by mail, but here goes. The ivy plants are dying. I'm not too sure about the health of the jade plant either, now that I think about it. The scraggly dried up strawberry begonias that you said I could have are flourishing (you can have them back when you return) and the struggling philodendron looks as if it might make it, but I think the ivy feels abandoned.

I'm really worried about it. I've never gotten along well with ivy in the past. I know I should have told you that when you asked me to plant sit, but I assumed you didn't want to split them up with you gone and I didn't want to complicate your departure.

Kathy, I'm worried, not about you. I'm sure you can take care of yourself out there in the jungle, but what about the ivy, here in my dining room?

Perhaps I need more explicit instructions. It seemed so simple and straightforward when you left them off. What should I do? Write soon. O.K? What do you usually feed them? Could they be homesick? They miss you terribly!

So do I!
Edee

DAILY DOINGS

February 13, 1978

Dear Sis,

I agree. Job, family and household are hard to juggle. I don't know if anyone ever gets used to it. I'm lucky. My kids are pretty self-sufficient. At our house the morning goes in shifts. The kids take care of themselves. Which is great, because in the morning it's all I can do to get *me* out of bed and on the road. (Morning ought to come later in the day when I'd be up to handling it.)

Eldest's bustling about occurs earliest. At some point she says, "Bye, Mom." That's my signal to swing into action.

Feet on the floor. Logs on the fire. Water in the bread pans (homemade humidifier). Clothes on the body. Start the car. Log on the gas pedal. Go in. Wake son. Put water jug in the car. Sweep snow off the car.

Drive, very carefully, to work. (I forgot my lunch.) Arrive. Plug in the car. Work. Check plug-in at noon, no lunch anyway. Work. Approach car. Hold breath until glow of engine heater light comes into view. (More than once I've had to plug in again and start waiting at quitting time. That's no fun.)

Start car. Fill water jugs. Sweep off car. Begin journey home. Grocery shop. Stop at post office. Drive. . . . Zap!

Two, count them, two bright red indicator lights say Toyota feels taken advantage of and wants a day off.

Gamble. Drive to my favorite service station—the one that offers moral support as well as reliable mechanical attention and takes my credit card to boot. They ask, "Can you leave it?" Do I have a choice? How about waving a magic wand instead?

Call kids to say I'm busy having car trouble, don't know when I'll be home. Eventually water jugs, groceries and I get a ride with a sympathetic mechanic. (Thanks, Greg.)

Arrive home on the rampage, as usual. Complain that Eldest hasn't shoveled snow. Scold Son for not splitting wood. Hassle Middle Child because indoor wood supply is exhausted. Harass them all because I am exhausted. (I don't know why they keep me.)

Put away groceries. Fail to appreciate daughters who fed selves rather than disturb me. Empty water jugs. Ignore son who hasn't eaten, but isn't complaining. Set sourdough for tomorrow's breakfast. Neglect to compliment Son on excellent job on dishes. Feel guilty for not fixing a hearty family meal.

Call around for a ride to work. Consider vacuuming. Eat lunch for dinner. Wonder what Son ate. Must have been something he shouldn't have because he cleaned up after himself.

Should make yoghurt for girls' lunches. Must plan what to wear tomorrow, can't think in the morning. Should fix tomorrow's lunch. Skip it. Probably forget it anyway.

Feed fire. Fill bread pans. Tuck in Young Son. Tell girls good night. Should. . . .

Phooey. Too many shoulds, musts and oughts in my life. Rather write to you. Wish I had an indicator light that told *me* when to quit.

> Good night in a hurry from your,
> Busy Big Sis
> me

TO SKI OR NOT TO SKI

February 20, 1978

Dear Mom and Dad,

No, I was not joking. I really am taking up downhill skiing. Middle Child and I have gone twice now, in self defense. It is the only way we could arrange to see The Eldest and Young Son on weekends. Actually, our interest began as a labor dispute. Half the household work force was too busy or too tired to work on weekends. We decided to go on strike as well. You might say the family that skis together sees each other, though the vacuuming never gets done.

The outcome is spectacular! We ski at the friendliest place you can imagine. Just being there is a joy!

It is open to the public, but is like a very, very exclusive country club. Membership does not depend upon how well you can ski, money, gear or social position. It's far more elite than that. The sole determining factor for whether or not you are welcome there is that you be a super nice person, kind, considerate, cheerful, fun-loving, friendly, etc., etc., etc.

For example, here I am stumbling my way down the hill. (No, it is not impossible to stumble on skis. I am getting quite good at it.) Strangers swosh past me at a nice safe distance and call out, "Looking good!" "Nice going!" or some other encouraging comment.

In fact, both days that we have been there someone has said to me toward the end of the day. "You sure don't give up easy." Isn't that nice! Or is it?

Skiing where the kids and all their friends ski is a mixed blessing. They are all excellent skiers and extremely eager to assist. Each time one glides down the slope they skid to a snow-spraying stop at my side. (Oblivious to the fact that I am terrified they will ski through me. I just don't understand how they stop those slippery things so suddenly.)

At my side they say, "You're doing great! Try this." Then they fly off down the hill leaving me to gaze at their graceful forms and wonder what it is I'm supposed to be trying. If it was to stay up, that is exactly what I *was* trying when I landed.

That's not the only help I receive. As each of these tutors passes me going up the rope tow they call out helpful advice like, "Remember, weight on your downhill ski." "Lean forward." "Bend your knees." "Plant your poles."

I will tell you one thing. I know I've gotten a whole lot better, because last week each and every time these encouraging comments diverted me I fell flat on my rear. This weekend, several times I was able to remain upright and merely lose what I loosely refer to as "control." Thus ski off into the bushes where I then got a chance to practice my kick turn.

Actually, I don't have as much trouble getting down the hill as I do getting back up. There is this Chinese torture device called a rope tow. It's designed to intimidate beginners, causing them to consider whether or not they really want to pursue this madness called skiing. If I don't get any closer to mastering that snake next week than I have so far, I am going to ask if I can bring an ice axe and cut stairs into the side of the mountain.

Wish me luck,
Dee

MONDAY BLUES

February 27, 1978

Dear Sis,

Here I sit in the laundromat trying to think of ways to cheer myself up. Surely there is no more odious task in the whole wide world than doing the laundry. What can I do to brighten up the chore?

Suppose I waltzed in one night smiling! ? ! Now that right there is enough to blow everyone's mind. A smile in the laundromat! What next? I'd even go further. I would say right out loud, something like, "Oh, how I do *enjoy* doing the laundry." I'd sing, be pleasant, the whole nine yards.

Imagine the looks of disbelief and astonishment, the gasps, the skepticism. People would move away from me suspiciously. (Hey! That's one way of getting enough machines, driers and clothes-folding space on a crowded day.)

Trouble is, I'd probably have to do the laundry at a different establishment each time. The management would assume I was a dingbat and try to discourage my presence.

A little earlier tonight a happy gentleman bounded through the door announcing proudly that he had managed to go three whole weeks between washes. A mere amateur. Soon enough the reason for his good humor was evident. He was dropping off his children so that *they* could do the laundry.

Three weeks? Pooh. I'd go three months if I could. My crew just starts complaining at about three weeks. (I hope they never get wise to the fact that there is no way we will ever do the laundry until *I* run out of clothes.) I worry that they might start hiding my underwear to instigate washday.

Often in circumstances of severe distress, sufferers develop a sense of comradery—We're-all-in-this-together-let's-make-the-best-of-it.

Well then, I ask you, why, amid the heat of the driers, the hum of the washers and the squeaky tires of the wire baskets do otherwise pleasant human beings become angry mothers, fussy babies, obnoxious pre-schoolers, surly children and stern spinsters? SOMETHING makes you jumpy. The competition?

The noise? The heat? The guilt of wearing the same socks so long in an attempt to delay the inevitable?

Tonight, about the seventh time I got hit by a wire basket doing a wheely, I jumped aside and stepped on the fingers of a creepy crawler. I cringed. Aghast and apologetic, I leaned over to comfort the babe, only to discover that he was a 14 year old searching for quarters in the cracks between the machines.

The chore is exhausting and befuddling any time of year, but during the winter when these horrendous glaciers form on the insides of the doors, I get frightened. What if the doors got frozen shut and I had to stay over night? Being held prisoner in a fortune cookie factory indefinitely would be sheer bliss compared to spending just one night confined to a laundromat.

Oh! Gracious! I have every single bit of household bedding and absolutely all of our clothes with me. The kids would be a whole lot worse off than I would if I couldn't get out tonight. I'd better hurry up, finish up and scurry home before that ice freezes.

Happy washday,
Sis

WINTERS MARCH ON

March 6, 1978

Dear Grandma and Grandpa Turner,

Remember the winter that your grandson broke his leg the *first* time? In late February, after months of miserable suffering the weather was suddenly splendid. We rushed out for a Sunday ski and crash!

Abruptly our very active five year old became a bulky blob to be lugged from place to place. To complicate a difficult situation the thermometer took a quick flip from 30° above to 30° below. That 60° turn plunged us into March like a polar bear.

Then the thermometer did not go above zero for what seemed like forever. One not too funny response to the constant question, "Will spring *ever* come?" was "Oh, did you miss it? That week in February *was* spring."

"Remember-the-winter-that. . . . " stories are stock up here, a standard way to indicate how long you've been around.

All of us seem to have total recall for one winter—the first one. Newcomers are more sensitive to life in the frozen north. I know a man who each and every morning of his first winter went out in his shirt sleeves to fully experience the drop in degrees. To this day he is an excellent resource person if you want to know what the weather of '66 was like.

After a few years though, memories of the wretched weather tend to blend. Instead, significant events highlight the years. Remember the winter the moose came out of the woods to beg for groceries off the kitchen table. Remember the winter the folks came up for Christmas. Remember the winter the leaves remained on the trees. Remember the winter we moved into the house. Remember the winter . . ., and so forth.

It's true though that one person's memorable winter is apt to be another's ruined routine. I remember the winter I worked with a merry dog musher. In February she took off on a dogsledding trip and when she returned in March to a slushy, early spring she was indignant. "This just isn't fair!" she complained. "They owe us another month of winter."

This intriguing attitude caused me to remember the lovely weather, but not the message. After that, in spite of the year of the broken leg, March meant mellow to me. So last year we planned our return from the sunny beaches of Mexico to coincide with my mythical "mushy" March.

Wending our way up the Alaskan Highway we met sub-zero temperatures amplified by a roaring windy chill factor.

Upon our return, at the very end of March (spring?), the splendid mild weather that we'd heard so much about via the national press and the U. S. mail service verified my skepticism by dipping quite close to 30° below. Not nice, Mother Nature, when one is living in a strictly summertime house on wheels. Well *I* remember that well, although that particular part of last winter seems to have slipped the minds of everyone else.

I notice, however, I am not the only one who is cautiously

silent about the weather we're having. February went out like a lamb this year, and the weather is wavering. I will go so far as to say that we are "sheepishly" waiting to see what March might do.

> Until spring,
> Edee

SUPERSUPERSTITIOUSNESS

March 13, 1978

Dear Tom,

I was going to write a silly letter to you about the mishaps I've been having with the Toyota, but I got cold feet. Figuratively.

Lately, I've been having some strange experiences relative to letter writing. It is almost as if someone has been reading my mail. Perhaps there is more to the power of the pen than I had realized.

In one letter I tossed off a light comment about needing more exercise. Next time I got on the scale I discovered five extra pounds.

In the midst of the severest cold this winter, I wrote to the folks that we wanted 20° above for Christmas. We got it! That wasn't hard to take at all, but it did confirm my childhood suspicion that Daddy is Santa Claus.

I complained about our time and temperature signs being inaccurate and as if by magic they started running like clockwork.

Then I joked by mail to some friends about how much I missed power outages and we started having them. That's not funny.

I realize that you don't think it's sensible to attribute human characteristics to vehicles, but really, Tom, my experience indicates otherwise.

You've met my 27 1/2 foot bus with its enormous dual real wheels. Remember that the only flat tire in our entire 11,000 mile trip occurred on the winter-deserted Alaska Highway at a well-equipped service station when it was time for me to take a coffee break.

Now if that isn't consideration I don't know what is.

Back to the Toyota. The first time I ever thought it had compassion for me was shortly after I bought it. I left a party where during a discussion I had declared emphatically that some women are as strong as, if not stronger than, some men. When I went out I discovered the car was immobilized by ice.

I straightened the wheels, dug out from around the tires, and said, firmly and with feeling, "Listen, Toyota, under the circumstances, there is absolutely no way I can go back in and face those people. If you never climb out of a slick situation again, please, allow me to leave gracefully this time." Up, out and down the hill we sped.

It was the beginning of a very supportive relationship. (I support the Toyota and it does the best it can.)

The most recent evidence of sympathy that I can offer included the law. Earlier this winter the light switch developed a quirk which left me with high beams or no beams. Days were dark on the way to work and on the way home. I'm sure I annoyed a lot of people. (My apologies to you all.)

Each time someone indicated to me that my high beams were bothering them I cut to no beams to show what the problem was. It was inevitable that one of my explanations would strike a policeman. It did. We had a talk. I explained that the switch was "on order." It is. He sternly suggested that I speed up order of said switch and sent me on my way.

I was only mildly upset, because I knew I was doing the best I could, but the Toyota! ! Tom, you don't have to believe this, but it *is* true. Since that evening the Toyota's lights have worked perfectly.

'Nuff said?
Dee

FOR MARCH 23

March 20, 1978

Dear Sweet Birthday Girl,

BEST WISHES! and CONGRATULATIONS!

Congratulations on being so soon, a straightforward, outspoken and principled young woman with:

—a spirit of adventure;

—a lively imagination;

—an awareness of the wonder of the world;

—a high regard for friendship;

—a good grasp of the fact that you and you alone are responsible for your moods, your success, your happiness and any disappointments you may suffer;

—a certainty that *your* way is the right way for you even if it doesn't fit in with everyone else;

—a sense of values based on honesty, fairness, trust, good judgment and respect for yourself and others;

—an understanding of the importance of solitude and the ability to enjoy your own company;

—a concern for, sensitivity toward and appreciation of people of all ages;

—and enthusiasm for books, dance, music and poetry.

In short, Dear, congratulations on being a very fine person at an early age.

Best wishes too. Good luck on achieving all your big and little goals now and always, but right now special luck on the ones we've talked about:

—living life on your own terms;

—being treated like a human being;

—learning to use your stubborness wisely now that you've discovered its usefulness;

—harnessing the ups and downs of growing up;

—becoming more tolerant (May I suggest that you too are part of the population that deserves your tolerance.);

—traveling far and wide;

—finding an exciting career.

Remember, Sweet, that you are a unique and wonderful being, as is every other creature on this earth. In addition to our splendid individuality, all of us are quite similar inside. Those deep, dark secrets that you harbor silently are the very things which worry others too. Share. Care.

Remember that we fear the unknown for good reason—to prepare us to deal with what emerges from the "darkness." "Fight or flee," but don't become immobilized. The choice is up to you.

Being alive is a privilege and a joy. Don't let life just happen to you. Help it along. Think big. You can do whatever you want to do. It's up to you.

The "Mother's Manual" says I should offer you mountains of advice, but all I can think of is:

STAND STRAIGHT. HOLD YOUR HEAD HIGH AND SMILE.

Oceans of Birthday love and much of the everyday kind too,

Mom

P.S. Incidentally, Jill Katherine, I like you *very* much.

AN ANNIVERSARY?

March 27, 1978

Dear Sis,

A year ago yesterday we reached home after our splendid winter of travel. Remember how determined I was to sell out, pack up and move south? Today I finally realized what everyone else figured out a long time ago. I'm not leaving Alaska. I live here.

All along I said I wanted to move south because life would be "easier" down there. Whatever made me think I like things easy? Hassle makes life more fun.

The extremes and dramatic changes we have up here are life-spicers. They help one appreciate the wonderful world we live in.

How often do people in Texas or Florida thank heaven for a few more minutes of daylight?

It has been a lousy winter for those who live up here because they like to pat themselves on the back for being hardy, rugged and resourceful. It's been nice. Mild, pleasant, enjoyable weather can be a real disappointment. There's just no struggle required.

Having a "warm" winter *has* made coping with life in the frozen north a whole lot easier than usual. It has made appreciating this place easier too. For one thing, you can see. Our vision is unobstructed by ice fog, iced-up windshields, ruffs and hoods. We even have our wolf ruffs turned back as if they were for decoration rather than survival!

The truth is, I *like* winter. (Which is easy to say when temperatures have been above $0°$.) Crisp, cold air perks me up. Frost on the trees is a marvel. Crackling wood fires make my day. Snow fascinates me coming down and piling up. I enjoy walking in it, skiing on it and moving it around. (I don't like getting stuck in it, but there's plenty of challenge to that as those who helped me out of the ditch last weekend will attest.)

There isn't enough room down where you are, Sis. I was fascinated when we moved from California to Colorado with the fact that towns had edges. When you left one town to go to the next one there was wide open space between them! ! ! ! Here when you leave one town it's hard to find the next one. That kind of space feels good.

The other kind of elbowroom that means a lot to me is the kind that people allow. There is a premium on that up here. "You do your thing. I'll do mine. I may not understand or approve, but I respect your right to be and do what you believe." That attitude pretty much leaves the rest up to the individual.

So this shoot of the family tree is growing roots and branching out. Having traded my slab wood kitchen for cabinets with doors and a counter top, I guess I'm pretty serious about spiffying up this shack and calling it home.

I miss you and I'm sorry that I won't be closer to you, but I belong here.

Bis Sis

© 1979 W. D. Berry

H$_2$O

Dear Sis,

To answer your question decisively, it all depends. Ordinarily I don't mind hauling water at all. It's just a necessary nuisance like making the bed and setting the table. I don't think much about it.

Until someone says: "You *carry* your water? *How* do you manage? ! ?" Instantly the chore becomes a tribulation, a burden. I question my motives. I consider the possibility that I harbor some sick inner need to suffer deprivation and distress.

I search my conscience. I re-examine my priorities. Am I warping the children by requiring them to heat water before doing the dishes? Is it cruel and unusual punishment to expect them to empty the slop bucket? (They think it is.) Is it unreasonable to take them swimming so many times a week just to get them clean? I wonder.

Certainly I would feel funny down there in an ordinary subdivision lugging my 5 gallon water jugs up the sidewalk from car to house. However, since some of the water that comes out of the ground in our town is so full of minerals that it clinks when it hits the sink, jug hauling is common in the nicest neighborhoods. We don't necessarily have sidewalks to steady our step, but then civilization is measured on a different scale in these parts.

Anyway, enough people I know do without ordinary plumbing facilities that a few years back when a friend was trying to organize a noon meeting he turned out to be the only person unable to attend. The rest of us, all women, regularly spent our noon hour in the same place—the gym shower. When we met him on the steps after we had cleaned ourselves, we filled him in on what we'd discussed. Though no one had taken notes.

Given the socializing that goes on in community showers, I suspect people have a basic urge to gather at the river for their cleansing ritual. (Our river is not exactly a convenient place to bathe.)

One limiting aspect of indoor plumbing is that you tend to

miss many fantastic auroras if you have no reason to go out-doors on a winter evening.

Yes, there are certain common characteristics of water haulers. One arm is apt to be longer than the other or both arms might be exceptionally long. They tend to gasp audibly and wince when someone pours a full glass of water, takes two sips and empties the rest down the drain. They get panicky when water is left running. They are over-eager about helping with washing chores in settings provided with hot and cold running water and display unnatural pleasure in the task.

Why do I do it, you ask. On occasion I ask myself the same question. The answer is fairly straightforward. I can't afford anything else. However, all things are relative. I have a friend who doesn't have water or a car. She doesn't haul water, she melts snow. For the life of me I can't imagine how she manages.

Must sign off and go water the plants. They are looking exceedingly thirsty. They suspect I'm complaining about how much they drink.

Dee

BLEH! APRIL, WHO NEEDS IT

April 10, 1978

Dear Sis,

How are you? I've got the blahs and I'm blaming it on April. It is possible that the reason the IRS moved taxtime from the Ides of March to the middle of April was because April had so little going for it. Up here every other month has something to recommend it, some personality or redeeming feature. Not April, it just takes up space.

March offers the promise of spring, a teeny, tiny tease. The calendar says yes, the climate says NO WAY, but wait . . . maybe. February is brief, but sweet, and somehow always manages to provide a show of splendid weather as if determined to boost our morale when we need it most.

January is dreary, dark, cold and predictable, but we all know we're gaining daylight and that balances the dismal. December has Christmas and doesn't have to do anything else to justify its position on the calendar.

November is generally miserable and that certainly is a definitive personality, though it might not be the type you'd prefer to pal around with.

October has two faces—the joy of fall and the exhilaration of the return of winter. In a land where winter is what life is all about that first burst is a welcome reunion. Guess my Libra orientation colors my attitude toward October too.

September is brilliant FALL as only birch-covered hills can play it. (Given a choice I'd opt for two Septembers and no April.)

August is hot or rainy, flip a coin. Rainy is quite all right, because we don't see enough of that kind of water around here to get tired of it. Mud puddles that come from the sky instead of the snow are a welcome change.

July is hot. Hot, dry and dusty. Summer. June is the introduction of summertime. Kids are out and about. Plants are in the ground. Nights go on forever. May is Spring! The world is changing dramatically, drastically and fast. There is promise. Summer is ahead.

April just sits there, like TV re-runs done in a random pattern. All other months have something to complain about, too cold and dark or too hot and you can't sleep because of the light. It's so dry your skin stings and you can't see for the dust or it's so wet the ditches absorb passing cars. There's too much snow or not enough. (Too much on the driveway, not enough on the slopes.) We're impatient for break-up, then we complain about puddles and mud.

Coping is easier when there is something to combat or enjoy. April doesn't offer either. It isn't warm enough to be comfortable or cold enough to be miserable. April showers and spring flowers don't exist up here. Although, during the day there is a constant stream dribbling down the *inside* of the south wall of my livingroom.

A leaky roof! That's what April has to offer. Maybe Mother Nature wants us to holler "Uncle" so she knows we appreciate spring when we see it. Hey! I've discovered April's function! Jan., Feb., Mar., Uncle, May., June, etc.

I'll write more later when I'm in a better frame of mind—in May. Meanwhile do enjoy an April shower for me that comes down on the outside rather than the inside.

Much love,
Sis

DRIP-DRIP-DRIP

April 17, 1978

Dear Mom and Dad,

I don't want to go out and finish shoveling the roof. I really don't. To make matters worse the temperature is just below freezing so the leaks aren't nagging me. Yesterday the drip-drip-drip drove me up to the roof.

I can't complain about the problem too much. When we put the roof between us and the sky it was November of a good, cold, early winter. We were preoccupied with keeping snow off the floor and didn't think too much about what would happen once it piled up overhead.

Can you relate to puddles hanging from the ceiling? Imagine lying on the couch and looking up to see the ceiling studs stuffed with foil-backed insulation covered with clear plastic (vapor barrier, right). Now do a double-take, because many of those saggy spots appear to be filled with substantial pools of H_2O. Hey, wait a minute! They really *are* puddles! ! Got it?

A vapor barrier is not actually applied for the purpose of holding puddles up in the air, that's just a fringe benefit of the system.

I claimed the "dampness" was condensation re-entry (a common Northern problem) for a few gallons, but once I was able to quit hauling water I had to admit that something was wrong. (I know I've always wanted running water and now that I've got it I'm complaining.)

I naively assumed that a little nestegg I'd been fostering was going to hatch into a lovely cedar ceiling. As the carpenters stepped into the livingroom to estimate the cost, they noticed the waterfall. Maybe it was the pots and pans around the room or the ping-drip-plop, but at any rate they noticed.

They did some calculating, consulting and calling around and reported back to me saying, "You need a roof."

"Ceiling, you mean." I said hopefully.

"Roof." Came the firm reply.

It seems that the moderate pitch of the roof counterindicates the covering material. In other words, it leaks. I *want* a ceiling. I need a roof.

Let's look at the bright side of the issue. Considering how much time I have spent up there patching and shoveling it is a good thing that the slope isn't any greater than it is. I might have fallen off. My snow removal style is more stomp, push, shove than shovel.

I stomp to break up the ice, give it a good shove with my foot to send it sliding down the incline and then sweep it the rest of the way. Too often I get carried away (literally) and my stomp sends ice, boot, foot and leg flying. Only the excellent braking power of my levi pockets keeps me from following my calving mini-glaciers over the edge.

However, stomping the roof is a very invigorating and satisfying activity and I am extremely glad that I have experienced this thrilling and chilling aspect of life in the frozen (and thawing) north. How's that for positive thinking?

Actually, Dad, what I'm writing for is to ask you if I could borrow some money so I can get a new roof *and* ceiling. I figure with a part-time job as a roof stomper I could pay you back in a hurry.

Anxiously awaiting your reply,
Dee

LET'S PLAY BALL!

April 24, 1978

Dear Wednesday People,

Would you believe I'm hooked on volleyball?! I can't believe it. One of my most vivid physical education memories from high school is cringing as two teams of volleyball players quarrelled about me. "No! You take her! We got stuck with her last time."

How humiliating! A "junior coach" (A position achieved because I was reliable, a qualified life guard and available.) rejected by her class. Customarily junior coaches were energetic athletes. That year they ran out of good candidates and used me.

For decades I have stood by my vow of, "Never, but never, in my entire life will I ever submit my psyche, soul and physical being to that form of torture again."

Many's the picnic, barbeque, beach, playground, gym, neighbor's yard and even dancehall where I have firmly answered, almost shouted, "NO WAY! ! !." I've lost some friends and made a few enemies with my hysterical reply to an innocent, "Hey, ya wanna play ball?"

Imagine my horror when, while getting acquainted at a brand new job, one of my colleagues-to-be bounded toward me with a cheery, well-meant welcoming gesture. You guessed it.

I have since apologized for my reflex response and admitted that I was excessively harsh and cruel, but I haven't yet figured out how I ended up out there on the gym floor. Out there on that court with my head spinning as I tried to keep track of a ball that wouldn't hold still and stay out of the path of all those people charging around.

I can only assume temporary insanity is what got me into that game. There is, however, no doubt in my mind about what keeps me going back. I am playing with the good guys. I am playing with an entire room full of people whose way of life revolves around positive reinforcement.

When I first began playing, if the ball came anywhere near me and I even looked as if I wished I had tried for it, some kind soul would shout a sincere, "Good try, Edee." Well, of course, the next time I *did* try. "That was a hard one, but you almost got it," was music to my ears. Then when I finally did hit it, "NICE RETURN! ! ! ! ! !" was the exclamation.

It didn't seem to matter that the ball ended up in the shower room and had to be dried off before we could continue. "We needed a breather," was the explanation.

All that encouragement is magic! Bumbling, stumbling old me, after all these years, is learning to play ball. I've taken an interest in the rules and sometimes even find myself wondering what the score is. I'm putting much less energy into hoping the ball doesn't come my direction. I even bought a pair of bright blue sneakers.

The exercise is invigorating, but that's a fringe benefit. What really feels good is those once a week loud and caring shouts of acceptance. I just wish that simply everybody had a chance to play ball with our team.

Thanks, You Guys, from,
Edee

THEY'RE BACK

May 1, 1978

Dear Marie and Jack,

We have a special spot in Fairbanks where birds, ducks and geese stop to rest on their way north from wherever they spend the winter to where they plan to spend the summer. You might think we are north enough, but most of the winged ones are headed on up to the Minto and Yukon Flats.

Viewing those areas from the air, it's easy to see why water fowl would want to spend time there. Miles and miles of lush, green, swampy, marshy ponds and lakes are entwined by rivers that meander around spilling over their edges and moistening the surrounding vegetation. A paradise for water fowl.

But what keeps them coming back each year to the same brown field in the midst of civilization at the edge of a busy street? From our perspective it is a scenic spot complete with a picture postcard barn and rolling hills in the background. Viewed from the sky, by a goose, what do the aluminum roofs, asphalt parking lot and muddy field suggest?

In years past I assumed that there was a scientific, esoteric reason why the flocks consistently grace this particular field. This year I pursued the question and was informed that our visitors are far more down to earth than one might expect. It seems that they choose this spot to stop because the accommodations are first rate.

You've heard the chatter that comes from those lovely chevrons in the sky. Imagine the conversation as a formation cruises along. A weary one speaks up, "Isn't it about time to pull over for awhile?"

"Where? I haven't seen a decent duck pond since we left home."

"Well, I remember there is a large open field not too far up ahead where the snow is always gone at this time of year."

"Oh, I remember that," comes a quack from the rear. "It's easily visible from the sky. There is a shiny slanted surface with even black marks on it. You can't miss it, even at this speed and altitude."

"Last year the Pintail's stayed there and enjoyed it immensely. The service is excellent, the food superb. Grain is specially spread and tasty as can be."

"What about creatures with thunder sticks?"

"There are some nearby, but they seem to be quite harmless. A fenced area limits their grazing and though they peer through various black devices toward the field, one has never been known to attack."

"We've met some White-fronted geese who return there every year and they believe that the two legged creatures actually welcome their arrival."

"That seems unlikely, but it's worth a try. We'll land and look it over. We don't have to stay if it isn't clean and comfortable."

The birds do come and stay and seem to enjoy themselves. Our cars and trucks, cameras and binoculars, picnic lunches and Brownie troops are ample evidence that we do enjoy the visitors.

Perhaps my interpretation is too frivolous. It could be that this is a serious gathering for the purpose of seeking to interest

94

the armed animals of the earth in the wonder of the airborne. If this is the case those lovely, graceful guests at Creamers Field are effective indeed.

How goes bird watching in New Mexico?
Edee

© 1979 W. D. Berry

LETTER WRITING ISN'T EASY

May 8, 1978

Dear Sis,

Let me see if I can explain to you why I don't write more often. Letter writing is very time-consuming and can be a great deal of hard work. I realize that all you ever see are paragraphs on a page, so I'll give you an example of what is involved in getting them there.

As I sit at my desk, ready to write to you, the sight of an unanswered letter from Auntie Carolyn nags me. So I drop her a pretty postcard saying that I'll write as soon as I can spare a minute. Then the date on the self-read electricity bill catches my eye—three days ago! I sprint out to read the meter.

On the porch four pairs of skis fall on me. They have fallen down at least once each day since the snow melted. I seriously contemplate building a ski rack right then and there. I begin rummaging for materials, but give up the idea when I realize I don't have the right size nails.

Back at my desk I write, "DEAR SIS, IT LOOKS AS IF SPRING HAS FINALLY ARRIVED." Which reminds me that I need to buy peat pots tomorrow and I want to know how many I already have. If I don't count them now I'll forget, so I go out to the shed.

There it is necessary to restack the studded tires which I just flung in there last week, pull out and fold up a super huge piece of visqueen and shove aside the odd pieces of insulation. I can't get to the pots through the clutter.

Once at my desk, I wonder what I had to say in the first place that prompted me to think I should write a letter. It seems a bit chilly so I consider whether turning on the furnace or building a small fire would be the most economical use of fuel. The carpenters left a bunch of lumber scraps around when they finished the roof. I go out to collect those for firewood. On the way into the house I hit on using my armload to make an impromptu wooden walkway along a particularly soggy spot on the path.

Washing my hands after my construction project, I notice

the water jugs need to be emptied into the 55 gallon drum and put into the car for refilling. At the car, I remember how impossible those dusty windshields were to see out of. When I come back in to get paper towels, I see the ingredients for yoghurt set out on the counter and make a mental note to take care of that and set the sourdough before I finish (finish?) the letter to you.

While I'm out cleaning the windows I hear my neighbor hammering. When I come in I call her to ask if she needs a hand holding a board or anything. We talk a bit longer than I'd planned. It's getting late when, after I've set the sourdough, made yoghurt and watered the houseplants, I get back to the desk to reread the "letter"—all 9 words.

Well, if I'm feeling loose I get up, pour myself a glass of wine, dash off a few quick thoughts and send you a message of sorts. If I'm feeling virtuous you don't hear from me. I chastise myself for not being more attentive to the task, for not being more concerned about you and for not composing a fascinating and cheerful epistle. Thoroughly scolded, I'm in too dreary a mood to write so I put it off until another day.

There's more to a letter than meets the eye, Sis. That's why you don't hear from me more often,

> But I'm thinking of you,
> Sis

THAT'S ROUGH

May 15, 1978

Dear Sis,

I'm too tired to write. I should send you an empty envelope full of sawdust. I poured myself a cup of tea, sat down to write a cherry little letter about sanding log walls and collapsed.

I think my body just went on strike.

I know I'm tired and too worn out to do much, but going to bed before 7:30 p.m. (alone) seems wasteful. I tried to knit, but my arms are still basically inclined toward the vertical and I can't get the fingers of my left hand to tighten down any further than the circumference of the sander-grinder.

Reading seemed logical, but I never could read while in motion and I'm still vibrating ever so slightly.

Letter writing it is. (Excuse the jer ky pen man ship. I think my trigger finger is trying to turn on the pen.) The reason that *you* rather than someone else will be the recipient of my literary efforts is that I can't think of anything nice to say.

I'm telling you, I feel as if I've been duped by the popular Alaskan myth that once you put up a log wall you are through, inside and out. Ho. Ho. Ho.

Next time I hear someone say, "Oh, we're building with logs. No more fussing with fancy finishing stuff for us." I'm going to smile, shudder and keep quiet. Let them learn the hard way too.

It all began when I had the ceiling covered (and that's not finished yet). A neighbor said, "What are you going to do to the walls?"

"Nothing." I replied. "I *like* rough lumber."

"And muddy foot prints on the wall and dust balls impaled upon splinters? and. . . ."

"What do you suggest?" I ventured, politely.

He brightened up. "I've got just the tool," He said. "It was used to grind pipe on the pipeline. It'll smooth down those walls in no time."

Seventy-two hours later, here I sit. I am in the sawdust, on the sawdust, looking through it, coughing it up, breathing it in and wearing it. Fondly I gaze at that magnificent machine. I've been a victim of a man's pride in his tool, but I agree. I have never seen anything that could so thoroughly wipe out an entire building. I can't even find part of the house.

This animal kicks, rears, bucks, growls, snorts and shoots sparks. It tore a hole in my new Levis and in my knee, but I hold no grudge. It is fast, efficient and thorough. The reason "we" took so long was not that the machine wasn't willing. It's just that I'm not able to hold that many pounds of active live weight over my head indefinitely anymore. It's been too long since the kids were little.

I wore goggles and a mask, but the goggles steamed up and between that and the cloud of sawdust it was often not easy to tell where I was going and where I'd been.

I'm done now though and guess what. A neighbor just stopped by and said, "Oh, how fine. What are you going to do to the walls now? Bleach them? Or stain them? Or. . . ."

Something tells me I'd better sign off before I go any further. I think my mind just gave out too.

Good night, I think I'll sleep soundly,
Dee

GUILTY AS CHARGED

May 22, 1978

Dear Sharron and Will,

Did I ever tell you that when I was 18 I was apprehended by a two-car, 8-man burglary detail for breaking into a service station? It was in the middle of a dark night at the edge of a big city. I vaguely recall the deafening alarm, screeching sirens, blazing lights and uniformed men emerging from every direction. I was calm. I waited to explain. I was innocent.

We had not broken into the service station. We had merely set off the burglar alarm by smashing into the garage door with a car we were trying to get started. (It had no brakes.) The fellows took off to test drive the finally functional vehicle and left me to explain the situation.

The squad car was quite crowded once I joined the men in the back seat. My interrogator was all business. He had a job to do—get the facts. His co-workers made it their job to put me at ease. They joked and teased. The discovery that my *occupation* was, college student, major—criminology, stirred up a lively discussion. But that is ancient history.

More recently, last week, at mid-day in a peaceful, sunny parking lot, at the edge of a lawn, I was apprehended by two uniformed military security persons. Noiselessly they glided up behind me as I was parking to go in to work. Solemnly they approached me and proclaimed, staring past me at my car, "We clocked you with radar— 21 mph in a 15 mph zone."

Redhanded! ! I trembled. I shook. I stuttered. My eyes burned. I opened my mouth, but no words issued forth. I wanted to run. At last I found my voice.

"I must go into the building and report." I stammered, scanning the horizon for an appropriate escape route.

"You can't leave." They answered icily.

"I must!" I insisted, sprinting toward the door. Inside, I hit the nearest water faucet, gulped eagerly, slumped against the wall and exhaled. After a few deep breaths, I marched myself right back out to face the ordeal, lecturing all the way. "Edith, you ran from the scene of a crime. You know better than that. Grow up. Accept responsibility for your actions."

All the while I kept wondering. Why am I so shook up? I've thought about that a great deal since then. Do I need more practice being bad and getting caught? I rejected that idea. Last time I got a ticket I was guilty, resigned to the inevitable and had a very nice chat with the policeman about all sorts of pleasant things. Fairbanks policemen are extremely nice guys.

That's it! These authorities acted like machines! I was apprehended by eyes that didn't see me, ears that didn't hear and a mechanical device I don't understand. I'm reasonably accustomed to being treated like a human being—guilty or innocent. I don't mind getting caught and justly punished. That's to be expected, but I also expect to be acknowledged as a living, breathing human being.

Come to think of it, perhaps it was my car they were speaking to and not to me at all.

Anyway, Mother will be delighted to learn that someone up here is keeping an eye on me. I've been put on restriction for thirty days. Same old punishment. I'm only allowed to go to and from work and classes. On restriction for the first time in 20 years, but at least this time it wasn't for missing lock-out.

Catch you later when I can travel faster,
Dee

JUSTICE FOR SLUGGARDS

May 30, 1978

Dear Mom and Dad,

This is the week of the garden in Fairbanks, Alaska. Like Alice's white rabbit in Wonderland, I've been racing around scolding myself all the while. I'm late. I'm late. The very important date that is mocking me is tomorrow.

Just as certainly as Christmas comes on the 25th each year, the garden *must* be quietly, placidly in place and growing by May 31st. At 11:59 p.m., on that particular date, the dust settles and vegetables and flowers-to-be all over town begin to grow in unison.

There is a popular belief that things that are not in the ground by June 1st won't grow at all. I shall soon find out, because in my shabby little brown plot last year's frozen vegetables are still lying in crumpled heaps under the winter's ashes—undiscovered corpses on a forgotten battlefield.

They haven't been plowed under yet because I'm waiting. Waiting for fresh, healthy dirt which is on order, but hasn't arrived. Waiting for the loan of a pick-up truck with an owner who has good feelings about manure. Waiting for a rental rototiller to be free. So that I can furrow, burrow, hoe and sow, hoping plants will start to grow.

This year I'm even later than late. I have *dusty* window sills. Now that might not shock you, but every self-respecting Alaskan knows that during May it is mandatory that all available sunny surfaces be covered by peat pots. Moist, damp garden soil on the TV, around the telephone, in the oven and under your pillow signifies good clean living. Dirt on the window sill of any home is proof of planning, organization, good management and sound use of resources. In short, it means the inhabitants bought seeds.

Now I have a problem about seeds. They just don't turn me on. A 49¢ paper package with a faded picture doesn't appeal to me. It doesn't move or smell or radiate energy like a $1.39 a 1/2 dozen growing plants. Seeds just sit there.

Looking at those tiny things, I don't understand how anyone

can believe that they are really going to sprout wings and grow. I mean in the *dark* and in the *dirt* of all places. Get lost maybe, but grow? ! Highly unlikely.

Give me a sturdy little green stem and some bobbing bouncing baby leaves and I can imagine the beginning of a foot long zucchini, but how are those teeny weeny funny shaped hard things going to provide my family with leafy greens all summer? It just doesn't seem likely. In fact, the only "seeds" I believe in are potatoes and onion sets. They make sense. Plant an onion, get an onion.

Spring has been early, lovely and warm this year. Some organized eager beavers put plants and seeds in the earth a little bit earlier than usual. A real no-no in these parts. How I envied them, last week.

However, this weekend Mother Nature offered her disorganized offspring (like me) some solace. She sent us snow on Saturday morning. What a joy to wake up, peer out of one sleepy eye and have the sky say, "You're not all bad, Lazy Bones."

Better sign off, I've got to go shovel some stuff and wash out a pick up.

How's *your* garden?
Dee

FRIDAY NIGHT FEVER

June 5, 1978

Dear Sis,

When will I ever wake up to the fact that everybody occasionally needs a little bit of fun in their life, especially me. All work and no play makes Jack a dull boy and me a miserable, ornery person.

I just ran across a quote that says, "Like money, time doesn't seem to go as far as it used to. . . ." Whole-heartedly, I agree! With the decreasing value of the minute, it is essential that each day be carefully organized. Therefore, I've been planning these elaborate weeks with every instant and activity arranged. At the end of each of these agendas I plot a Friday night which is designated as time for tying up loose ends or (get this bit of fantasy) starting out on the weekend's big new project.

Deep down inside I know the only one fooled by all this paperwork is me, but still I persist. Inevitably, at the end of a diligent week, I find myself on Friday night spent, bleary-eyed, and grim, staring at the designated terminal task.

Dimly in the echo of my memory I can hear mother saying, "Edith, it's time to give up. You've put the zipper in twice now, both times upside down. It's time to put the sewing machine aside. Start fresh on a new day."

The wisdom of the advice escapes me. There I sit, woebegone and bedraggled, confronted with the chore that my conscience and my schedule says I must attack. It doesn't matter what the chore is, on Friday night they all look the same—dismal.

Lifeless and fading, I flinch at the sound of the telephone. Wearily, I lift the receiver. "Hello?" I wheeze weakly.

"You sound awful. Did I wake you?"

"No." I sigh.

"Want to go dancing?"

"No. I couldn't possibly." I whisper. "I've got too much to do."

"To do! Ridiculous! It's Friday night! Pick you up in half an hour." Click. (My dancing buddies must have had more convincing mothers.)

What can I do? Swiftly I swing into action, get dressed and get gone. Eagerly I join the carousing crew. Tirelessly, well into the wee hours, I celebrate the end of the week with energetic people, good music and lively dancing. On Saturday morning I wake refreshed to face a new week.

When will I ever learn. Friday night is Weekend Eve, a time for wringing out the old and bringing in the new. A time to relax or party, dissipate or vegetate, socialize, nap or snooze, but not! No! NOT! NO! never a time for *doing* anything.

Next Friday night, right on my calendar in bold black letters I am going to put down—HOWL! It'll have to be next week because this Friday night I've got to grout the tile in the kitchen, write a letter to the folks, vacuum and. . . .

Oh, dear, there I go again. When will I ever learn? It takes some of us longer than others. No wonder I need to get organized. I'm terribly slow on the uptake.

Sis

52 WEEKS LATER

June 12, 1978

Dear Readers,

For almost two years the plan rumbled around in my head. Basically the idea was: We, the people of the great state of Alaska, are unique, unusual, charming and quick to see the humor of our plight—life in cold, dark, primitive isolation. We consider ourselves just a little bit different from anyone else in the world because we live here.

We may be wrong, but if we are we'll never know, because those who are eager to point out our insanity are also eager to leave and those who stay soon join our smug state of mind.

We ought to boast a bit of our prowess, to banter about the light and bright side of the dismal aspects of our special world, to justify (perhaps glorify) our presence here to ourselves and our friends. Just for fun. To do this in print, right out loud, would be good for morale.

For a couple of years, while taking notes, storing anecdotes and exercising positive thinking (the latter to maintain my sanity rather than with an eye to publication) I became more convinced that *someone* ought to expose what we really experience. Scores of clever people in our town could amuse us with a cunning version of life in the far north, but no one came forth.

Then all of a sudden someone was regularly writing what I had in mind, but that "someone" wasn't any of those clever people. It was me. Reality descended. Deadlines are demanding and unrelenting. Not all weeks *are* light and bright. Some days are better than others and others are just plain dreary. Thinking positive 500 words a week can be hard work.

At first I was uneasy. What if what I was saying was just super stupid? What if no one else up here considered ice fog, dark days, waffle stompers, or power outages worth reading about? What if. . . . but slowly questions and comments were heard. Proof at least that my letters were being read.

Answers were easy. No. I don't work for the newspaper. I've a full-time "other" job. I write letters in my spare time, just like everyone else, only once a week I try to make them suitable for general consumption.

Yes, the people I write to are real, but those aren't my actual letters to them. In fact, they have hardly heard from me since I started doing the column a year ago.

Yes, I do live the life I portray, only more so. Some of the gory details aren't exactly appropriate for print.

People were reading the column! They were paying attention! They understood! They agreed! I was prepared to be considered corny, but I hadn't fully appreciated how much of what I perceived would hit home solid for so many others.

Some weeks I get bogged down and wonder: What am I doing this for? Why don't I go home from work, fix dinner, do the dishes and *read* the newspaper like a sensible person. Then I call to mind the many nice friends and strangers who have stopped me in the grocery store or parking lot and said, "Right on, Edee! You said exactly what *I* feel about. . . ."

That reassuring feedback makes it possible for me to write on. Readers, what I want to say is—

Thank you,
Edee

PATERNAL LEGACY

Dear Pop, Dad, Daddy, Father, Hey You,

Happy Father's Day a day late and a dollar short. You know that if I ever amount to anything in the world of words you can claim a great deal of the credit. It was from you that I learned to appreciate and enjoy words. It was you who challenged me regarding spelling, pronounciation, meaning and nuances attendant thereto. (Did I do that last part correctly?)

I was the first kid on the block to know we went to the "library" not the "liberry" to pick up a couple of books. I remember practicing "am-*bu*-lance," "Fe-*bru*-ary," and "*k-war-t*er" instead of "core-der" for "quarter."

In the olden days when "antidisestablishmentarianism" was supposed to be the longest word in the dictionary I was the neighborhood resource person. Not only could I say it and spell it, I knew what it meant. All because of you.

Funny that I never minded having my letters red-penciled and returned by you. Believe it or not, I always took pains to correct the errors you detected. Last time I was down there you said I was doing better, but still had some pet mistakes that it looked as if I would never outgrow. Ever since then I've wondered what they are. (There's one of them, I'll bet. Is it "ever" or "every?")

After realizing that one of my standard *faux pas* is the way I spell "stomache" (The "ache" part makes perfect sense in view of how mine often feels.), I decided to keep track of the words I have to look up and try to analyze why they present problems for me.

Take "exasperated" for instance. When I'm in a frame of mind to use that one I'm feeling like "grrr" and I always assume it has at least a "g" or two in it. I'm certainly in no mood to look it up.

I can never remember whether "placid," which I definitely am not and never have been, has one "c" or two. (It still doesn't look right.) Since I have to look up "erudite" everytime I use it it probably doesn't apply to me. Though I never claimed to be

106

"ingenious" the big book offers the consolation that I might be "ingenuous" and I didn't even know it.

"Caribbean" only has one "r!" Now I'm sure that if I'd ever been there I'd remember that. As it is, on the rare occasion that I use the word I have to look it up to find out how to spell it *and* how to say it. I should travel more.

You always said that if I pronounce a word correctly I'd have a better chance of knowing how to spell it. "Calendar," which I can never spell, I pronounce "calunder" and "maintenance," which I spell "maintainence" but say "maint'nence," are excellent examples of that theory. (I never can figure out what letter to put where the apostrophe sits.)

I'm extremely careful about using both anecdotes and antidotes, because I'm never sure how to spell or say or what to do with either one of them. So it goes.

The point is, you might think I would take the easy way out and stick to short, easy words, but I've never given up my childhood dream of finding one word that *you* cannot spell or define. Although I know you've got it pretty well memorized, each time I go into the lexicon I hope that I just might find one vocable that has escaped you all these years.

Speaking of which, you taught me to calendar when I used to help you in the darkroom. Did you know that?

Live and learn.

> Love,
> Dee

STORE SUMMER SKYSCAPES

June 26, 1978
Lia's birthday!

Dear Auntie Carolyn,

Last night as I watched a "Big Bird" ease up off the runway to soar past grey clouds into a sunlit sky, I wondered how it might feel to be a visitor to our fair city going to the airport to take a late night flight in the sunshine. The day had been rainy and dark and the clouds were just breaking up to reveal a bright blue sunny sky, but it was *midnight.*

I'd gone down to mail something at the airport post office. I was in a gloomy mood and preoccupied. Tossing the envelope into the box, I thought, well now that's done, on to the next project. I turned around (this put me facing north) and WHAM-MO! The summer sky seemed to exclaim, You have forgotten about me!

It was right. In years past the summer sky has been a fascination for me, an inspiration. The summer I worked 11 p.m. to 7 a.m. as a janitor is one beautiful blaze of sky in my memory. I know for a fact that I spent plenty of time staring at dirty floors in fluorescent hallways, but it was magnificent sunsets and sunrises that kept me going.

The year I worked 5 p.m. to midnight as a cocktail waitress there was great comfort in turning occasionally from the dim light of the lounge to see that the sunshine was still outside waiting for me to get off work and come play.

These days (and nights), maintaining a sensible schedule, I'm missing the midnight skies and all they offer. I've always believed that our additional daylight supplies us with surplus energy so that we can overachieve in the summer, but I'm beginning to suspect it is necessary to *watch* the sky in order to absorb that change.

Those of us who spend the day indoors under stale electricity, staring at paper projects don't seem to be much more lively than usual. Maybe, just as plug-in power reassures us that we've nothing to fear in the darkness of winter it diverts our attention from the uplift of summer. There might be a bit of jealousy between the two sources of light, but there certainly is no comparison.

More than the illumination, it is the pageantry of the summer sky which is so captivating. Sunset and sunrise maneuver so precisely that an audience has just enough time between them to look from north to south and see the colors of the setting sun reflected on the Alaska Mountain Range. The jagged white peaks turn pink, peach or purple. Your neck can get tired trying to catch the slow dip, the reflection and the swift ascent of a pastel dawn.

If you work all day and go to bed at a reasonable hour you miss this spectacle. I have a dream that if regularly, in unison, in midyear at midnight the entire population of our town went outdoors to look up and contemplate the grandeur of our unique and incredible world, we could store up vivid memories of warm colors and fanciful undulating cloud formations to help us make it through the winter.

With practice and considerable mental effort we might then learn to simultaneously project these images onto the blanket of ice fog that surrounds us six months later and melt it. Such is the power of people, don't we wish.

Your loving niece,
Edith Carolyn

BY JILL KATHERINE TURNER

July 3, 1978

Dear Grandma and Grandpa,

Mom's too busy to write and so she asked me to tell you what's been going on in my summer. It started off with 23 miles of uphill down dale, rain, snow, hail and occasional sunshine. There was plenty of good healthy exercise, sore shoulders and bruised hips from pack straps and five days of magnificent scenery.

Where did we find this? Up in the mountains above treeline about 95 miles north of town at Eagle Summit. Lia, her best friend, Sarah, and I took to the trail by ourselves. To you 16, 15 and 14 might seem a bit young for such a trip, but we managed nicely.

The first night we reached Porcupine Dome. We thought. It wasn't, though, and after that we called everything larger than a molehill Porcupine Dome. The half-way point, Swamp Saddle, sure fits its name. There is no way we could miss it. I don't know about the saddle part (We were too wet to really notice the shape.) but it sure was swampy. We would step on a hump that looked fairly dry and sink to our knees in soggy squish.

Imagine our elation at reaching a lovely, solid, semi-dry boardwalk made of 12' long 2 x 10's about halfway through the swamp. Walking along, I began thinking of all the effort it took to get those huge heavy boards there. I mean, imagine carrying one of them on your back for 11 miles! So when the boards ended, although I was sorry to begin that weary sodden tramp again, I didn't mind *too* much.

When we sat down to rest I expressed amazement that all of those boards had been carried so far. As I was contemplating this wonder, my sister said, "Silly! Can't you see, they brought them in by helicopter."

One of the most well-used, beloved pieces of equipment was our tent. Someone said, "This tent is just like Old Faithful. It goes up, it comes down and it's always here when we need it."

Earlier, Sarah, the owner, said, "This tent was once dubbed the Best Arctic Tent for Morons." That's what we felt like often enough after a hard day of rain and wind on the tundra when all we wanted was to flop into a warm, dry tent and sleep. Instead we had to spend what seemed like hours standing around a tiny campstove in a roaring wind and occasional sprinkles waiting for water to boil. We would finally give up and dump the dinner in anyway.

The tundra appeared from a distance to be dull yellow or green, but it came alive when we examined it closely. We found thousands of different tiny, detailed plants, lichens, mosses and flowers in all shapes and colors.

Although we did have problems there was never a time when we wished we hadn't gone. It was stupendous! I felt big and small all at the same time. It was just me, the mountains and the sky. (Oh, yes, never forget the bugs!) The trail was the only thing linking my mind to cluttered city life.

At the end of five days and 23 long hard miles someone yelled, "Yahoo! ! ! ! We made it!" but it wasn't me. What I felt was a quiet sense of accomplishment.

I hope your summer is as full of excitement as mine is starting out to be.

Love,
Jill Katherine

SOME LIKE IT HOT

July 10, 1978
Dear Sis,

I'm lying here on my stomach feeling terribly guilty. I should be working. I should be weeding the garden, varathaning the ceiling and squirrel-proofing the eaves, but instead I'm lying in the sun feeling guilty. With any luck I'll get sunburned. That will serve me right for being so lazy. Isn't the work ethic great. If I got sunburned while weeding the garden I'd feel sorry for myself, but for restful sunbathing I consider the pain just punishment.

Actually I'm virtually certain to get sunburned, because I am winter white. We haven't had much sun. We've had a great deal of rain and during this month I have begun to suspect that I might be a positive thinker, or not very aware.

Once school is out I revel in every single moment of summer. So it surprised me one afternoon when a lady I was chatting with said, with no preface. "Isn't this bleak."

"Beg your pardon?" I inquired politely.

"This weather, isn't it awful."

I looked around, thought for the second time that day what a joy summer is in Alaska be it ever so brief and said. . . . Well, I don't remember what I said, but it wasn't appropriate and after that the conversation sort of lagged. Then I did say, I really had to run and drove off admiring the splendid thunderheads and wondering if the glum lady was having a bad day.

111

Several days later when a similar comment issued forth from an otherwise pleasant chap it started me thinking. Was I missing something? Didn't others enjoy the sound of rivulets splashing into rain barrels?

I was ready though when next I heard, "Isn't this weather awful!" I replied cheerfully, "A bit southeastern isn't it." (You have to know that Ketchikan, in southeastern Alaska, boasts about an annual rainfall of 154 inches to appreciate the tenor of that comment.)

"Beg your pardon?" came the reply. Very shortly the complainer found she really did have to run.

One day I decided to venture a more assertive response. "Actually I'm rather enjoying the fact that we're not having forty below." I mumbled hesitantly.

"We're not supposed to be having forty below!" Came the thunderous reply. "It's supposed to be hot!"

That's it! That's the answer. I don't like hot! Hot saps my energy, makes me drip, wears me out and slows me down. I like moderate weather. In fact, probably the only thing that I do like moderate is the weather. If I must choose between hot and cold, I'd rather have cold.

Cold you can get away from. You can build a fire, go inside, bundle up, even go to Hawaii. Hot follows you everywhere. Unbundling doesn't help. I don't know how to build an air conditioner. Inside is usually as hot or hotter than outside and going to Hawaii to escape Alaskan *summers* isn't in.

So here I sit, suspecting my skin is beginning to fry, trying to understand the psychology of the sun worshippers. Having accepted an invitation to sun, I was a bit reluctant to say, "Excuse me, but do you mind if I go indoors and knit?"

Instead, brightly, as I wiped my sweaty brow I commented, "Just think of all the natural vitamin D we're absorbing."

To which my companion answered, "Actually we're exposing ourselves to the possibility of skin cancer." That's when I decided to keep quiet and write a letter to you.

I'm ever so glad my favorite color is pink.

Sis

A GROWING EXPERIENCE

July 17, 1978

Dear Sharron and Will,

There is no doubt in my mind that I was not cut out to be a farmer. I've lost the potatoes. The instructions say: "Hoe up hills around potatoes when they blossom." I went out this afternoon to check to see if the potatoes had blossomed yet. (Blossoms, I'm pretty sure, I would have recognized as blossoms.)

However, other than the broccoli buds, which I suspect are deep down inside really flowers, nothing looked like a blossom or even vaguely familiar. That's not quite right. A whole lot of things look like broccoli, but I learned early on up here that those plants have a choice of being either cabbage, cauliflower, brussel sprouts or broccoli. You just treat them all the same until they decided what they want to be.

Actually they probably know in advance what they're going to be, it's me who keeps wondering. Reminds me of being pregnant. You spend nine months wondering about the outcome of something that was decided long ago.

Right now I wonder where the potatoes are. It's pretty clear to me that in the past where I put things when I placed them in the ground had a lot to do with my powers of recognition. I had a place for everything and everything in its place—right. I'm not an organic gardener, but I'm certainly an orderly one.

The problem is, I didn't put these plants in the ground. I'm sharing the garden with a friend. The arrangement is that he planted and tended til now and now I tend. Then I'll harvest. I suggested to him before he left town that he make me a map of what was what. I guess he thought I was kidding.

When my dad used to say "can't tell the cabbage from the lettuce without a program" I thought it was a joke. The joke's on me. I can't tell the cabbage from anything. The only thing I can recognize for sure is the visqueen and that's just because the kids picked it out of the salad the other night.

That's not quite true. Carrots I can recognize once they get big enough to thin and I always know I'm right, because I get to pull them up and check. Sweet peas, I mean snow peas are easy, because they look like sweet peas.

There are lots and lots of big healthy plants out there that I can't recognize at all, but I don't think they're potatoes. In fact, there is a possibility they're weeds. I weeded the lambs quarter the other day. Oh, goodness, I wonder how much a potato plant looks like chickweed?

Come to think of it. That doesn't help a bit either. This garden partner has gotten heavily into foraging and before he left he showed me all sorts of weeds I could eat while waiting for the garden to produce.

Who decides what's weeds and what's vegetables if you can eat both? Maybe if it's easy to grow (grows like a weed) it's not a vegetable.

By harvest time I have got to get this figured out, else how will I know what to write on the packages? Guess I could always label them at random and hope it takes him a long time to figure that out. Meanwhile, I'd better go look for the hoe. I'm positive I'll recognize that.

Hoefully yours,
Dee

JOINT TENANTS

July 24, 1978

Dear Chris, Tom, Cindy and Jennifer,

I just discovered the screen I had put up around the eaves when the roof was replaced because it leaked and the insulation was replaced because it was soaked and full of holes, dog food and spruce cones is not squirrel proof.

I've been suspicious all along because the squirrels didn't go away. A visitor assured me that, "You live in good squirrel country so there are bound to be plenty of them around no matter what." I told myself they were coming here to get supplies and running off to a new home. Boy, am I gullible.

It's not as if I feed them table scraps to lure them close. When the dog food is all gone they topple the tempting tops of the spruce trees and sit on the stump at the front door to dismantle them. Then they scold me when I walk past. If I startle them sufficiently they move a few feet away and read me the riot act for stepping out my own door at an inopportune moment. All this in spite of the fact that I've not once pointed out that they ought to sweep up after themselves.

From my point of view, as neighbors they are not all bad. As near as I can tell, they have this "we were here first and it's critters like you that cause a nice area to go downhill fast" attitude toward me. This is unjustified too. I'm basically the live-and-let-live type. (I'm the only person I know who shoos away mosquitoes and asks them not to bite.)

I'd like to put up wood around the eaves, but the 28 holes that need to be covered are 28 different sizes and shapes. Each one of those has various notches that have to be cut out. I tell myself this is proof that I have a very unique house. What it really means is that the carpenter won't touch the project. She says, "Edee, you can't afford to *have* that done." Translate, "There is no way I'm going to take on such a tedious and uninspiring task, even for money." Maybe I need a less creative, more mercenary carpenter.

I set out to cover up the opening where the squirrel was going in and out and as I was searching for logical lumber and contemplating the 7 little jogs that would have to be made in the basic 5 1/2" x 23" x 7 1/4" x 25 1/2" piece of wood I discovered their back door. I was about to be trained by a squirrel! Imagine the conversation:

"Bushy Tail, there is a draft coming into the nest from the northwest, should we move?"

"No, just tear a hole in the screen and that large, funny-looking two legged creature will scurry about making noise and block off the opening. I think I'd like the southwest side closed too. Once the 4-eyed animal is through fumbling around with the n/w corner we ought to tear a hole in the s/w." 28 times!

Peaceful coexistence is the only answer. I'll just think of them as the ideal pet. They don't ask to be let in or out or shed hair on the couch or require a sand box. The animal control people won't capture them and demand that I pay to get them back again.

Hey!! Wait a minute. I must close. I'm going to go see if my neighbor will call and complain that my pets are running loose, terrorizing the neighborhood and trespassing on her property. (With my luck they'll come get her squirrels and leave mine here.)

> More later from the nutty one
> in the family,
> Dee

TURN OF THE SHREW

July 31, 1978

Dear Sis,

Wow! This place creaks, echoes and squeaks. You would suspect a little "peace and nice" might be a pleasant change for a mother of three, but with the house empty I keep hearing ghosts—of me. It's unreal. I have this feeling that the kids arranged a feedback system of the nagging they usually hear.

Young Son is off fishing. The girls are both on a camping trip. The dog even wandered down to the neighbor kids for company. It's so quiet around here that I've started talking to the squirrels, mostly to drown out the realization of what a witchy mother I must be.

The first night they were all gone I used music to fill up the emptiness. Two cuts into the new Fleetwood Mac album I thought I heard a *very* familiar voice screeching, "That music is way too loud! Why do you always play music so loud?"

It sort of makes me feel less lonely, I thought sheepishly. (Ever wonder if the kids use volume to reorganize their space and not to annoy us after all? What a novel idea!)

The morning after they left I was picking at a bit of food and heard. "Buttered your toast right on the table! How crass! Use a plate or at least a napkin." Followed by, "You buttered it once, why are you putting more butter on it?" Picky, picky, picky.

In the course of the day I never did eat a decent meal. I countered the nags by insisting the absence of structured mealtime would be slimming. (Never have let them get away with that one.)

By 9:30 p.m. I was famished. I headed for the kitchen but could hardly get in for the blaring, ever so familiar, accusation. "Eating at this hour! Why don't you just go to bed? Why waste the groceries and calories? You aren't hungry, you're just bored. If you were hungry you would have eaten a decent meal at dinnertime."

But I *am* hungry, I thought, cringing at what I knew would be the reply. A standard since child number one was old enough to express herself, "Good! You'll eat a hearty breakfast. *Go to bed*!"

A little bit ago I realized I left my purse on the dining-room table, the mail on the credenza, my shirt on the couch and my shoes in the hall. There goes the voice again. "You have a room of your own. Why can't you take your belongings to your room before you drop them? Who do you expect to pick up after you? If you're going to leave things lying about that's fine, but do so in *your* own room!"

This efficient muzak of nagging has noticed that I: have consistently left the front door open; forgot to put the cap back on the toothpaste (In fact, I can't find it. May Young Son never find out.); cracked eggs and put the shells back in the carton; talked on the phone for far too long; ate all the ice cream without a thought of the others; put feet up on the couch with shoes on and many, many more transgressions that I consider the children uncivilized for committing.

I never would behave like this if they were home! I wonder if *they* are the ones who keep *me* in line. My kids may be mature enough to go off on their own, but it looks as if their mother can't behave herself without supervision.

Please don't breathe a word of this to your nieces or your nephew.

> Yours in secrecy,
> Sis

SITTING PRETTY

August 7, 1978

Dear Auntie Carolyn,

I am housesitting. In the olden days I used to collect mail, feed animals and tend yards for people who were gone for a week or two. Now I'm all grown up and I'm still doing it only the people are going away for a *month* or two. Someone is making progress.

I'm tempted to write a word to the wise for housesitters. I can see it now. First I would say: Anyone who needs a housesitter obviously has a reason for having the house sat—right? Don't think about it. Take my word for it. Now, in the winter that's pretty simple. The pipes might freeze. The cat needs food. The house plants must be watered. Very straightforward and easy to accommodate.

In the summer, however, *gardens* are the reason for "house" sitting. My advice is—don't do it. Pawn your belongings, auction off your children (or parents), hire yourself out for 75¢ an hour as a dart game target, but don't agree to take over a garden, a dog team, or a St. Bernard.

Houses will usually just sit there and be sat. Animals on the other hand, being social creatures, will want to introduce you to the neighbors and/or selected borough employees (as in animal control officers). Gardens require more TLC than any stranger can provide. (TLC stands for time, luck and courage.)

It is essential for anyone going into the sitting business to realize that no matter how conscientious you are about the agreed upon duties, the proprietors are going to be disappointed, because you didn't do what they would have done. Of course you didn't! You are only you.

It doesn't do any good, but it is wise to say in advance, "You must remember, I am only me." They will answer, because they are desperate, leaving momentarily and have a million details to deal with, "Oh, you will be perfect. Don't worry."

My advice is—worry. For upon their return it isn't what they say (at best a terse thank you), but what they think that gets you down. Oh, my goodness gracious, what they think, and to some extent with good cause. No matter how careful you are if *anything* can go wrong it will.

I have actually housesat in situations where: I hung out a rug to air and one side turned from a bright green to pale yellow, in spite of the fact that there was no sun where I hung it. In one house someone, apparently the cat, left a freezer door open and an entire year's supply of meat, fish, vegetables and berries defrosted into a puddle on the utility room floor. I was innocent! I only discovered there *was* a utility room when this colorful river oozed out from under the door and down the hall.

Here, just today, a tiny plastic bottle of some unknown substance fell out of the sky or some such place. I picked it up, put it on their nice new kitchen counter and instantaneously it ate a six-inch circle 1/4 inch deep into the formica. If the St. Bernard hadn't been guarding the door I would have run away and never returned.

There are many reasons for housesitting and they all end in "y." Economy (you are broke), generosity (they are desperate), courtesy (you can't say no), stupidity ('nuff said) and why. I qualify on all counts.

So who is in my house while I'm housesitting? No one. I know better. I'm straddling mine and theirs too. Theirs has running water and fresh green salad vegetables.

Your loving niece,
Edith Carolyn

SO MUCH TO DO
SO LITTLE TIME

August 14, 1978

Dear Sharron and Will,

Whoever markets the calendar should offer a two-for-one sale on days. I'm sure the idea would go over fantastically well in Alaska. In fact, even a two-for-one on hours would guarantee record sales. There simply isn't enough time to do everything there is to do in this town.

Remember when I first talked about moving up here from down there and you exclaimed, "What will you *do* in a small town way out in the middle of nowhere?" As if that's a problem. There's too much to do in this town. That's the problem.

Even a summer that leaves one deliciously unemployed doesn't free up vast expanses of unclaimed time, it just introduces umpteen options to pick and choose from.

There's the routine, unavoidable, homefront responsibilities and chores, plus the garden, which only takes up absolutely every single bit of time you'll give it and demands more. Blueberries are begging to be plucked already. So add picking, pies, muffins and jam into the daily dozen. Of course, we cannot neglect the standard non-specific socializing and visiting, else how would we know who is up to what.

Too often the temptation to tan a bit comes tugging too. I'm not very organized. I cram my day full of productive activity and end up ready to relax and sunbathe about 9:05 p.m. Even in the land of the midnight sun that's not a good time of night to lie about slathered with oil or lotion—unless it is Cutters or you're under the covers.

In addition to all of the ordinary activities, we have seasonal offerings that are basically tourist fare, but can be ever so much fun for the local to try. Right at the edge of town we have a miniature Caribbean cruise! We can take a ride on our rivers in a sternwheeler complete with spectacular vistas and entertaining commentary from a real life riverboat captain. Such luxury!

Then there is the city tour. I've always wanted to go on that anonymously. Like going to the zoo to watch the people. I'd like to listen to the travelers talk about our town. Tourists believe that they are up here to see Alaska. Actually we import them to freshen up our outlook on the familiar scene.

Another place, aside from our splendid museum, where we can observe these fascinated and fascinating specimens is a pioneer park near town, Alaskaland. It's a low key place to go and see things that are interesting, informative and fun, like tourists.

We've baseball to watch and all levels of all sorts of sports to participate in, plus at least three places around that every night offer old-timey fun and folly to watch and drink by. We must have more music per dancer and dancers per capita than any town alive, and this one is very lively.

That's just the daily menu. All summer there are specials like June's Summer Solstice when we celebrate the sun and July's

Fourth and special Days to commemorate the Golden past. Here is August already with Fairtime right this week!

I could go on and on, but I'm running out of time and space. Suffice to say, I'm not sitting around twiddling my thumbs.

> Gotta Run,
> Dee

RAINDROPS ON THE RUG

August 21, 1978

Dear Mom and Dad,

My house is getting to be so civilized that I hardly recognize it. The livingroom looks yummy enough to eat. The ceiling is finally in place, stained, varathaned and glowing the color of pouring honey. The purlins, cross ties (?), *round logs* (I always get those terms mixed up.) are smooth and shiny and look like pulled taffy. I just painted the floor a delicious caramel color.

Soon it's going to be difficult to convince myself I'm under-privileged. My next big dream is a real clothes closet to replace the pole in the corner, in the bedroom, not the livingroom.

I do so wish you would come up and visit this house you are helping to finance. It really isn't at all realistic for you to expect to wait until it's finished. Alaskan houses are never finished. They are like people, they keep on growing and changing forever.

You misunderstood about the running water aspect of the money I borrowed from you. It wasn't to *install* running water as in well, septic system, pipes and all that jazz. It was to *forestall* running water as in a leaky roof. Actually it didn't work. How many months ago did I have that done—the roof replaced? Still, every time it rains there are puddles all over the living room.

Every time there are puddles all over the livingroom, I call the roofer again. Often a lady answers. When I ask her to have the man call me, she says, "May I ask regarding what?" Every time I say, "A leaky roof." I have the feeling she thinks, "I'll bet," but that really is all we've got going.

Sometimes he returns the call. Sometimes he doesn't. Sometimes he sends someone out to fix the leaks. Sometimes he doesn't. Sometimes I get annoyed. Sometimes I don't, depending on how soon it rains again.

He's really very nice about it, but the roof still leaks. The main difference now is that with the ceiling in place you can't see puddles in the visqueen.

I wish you hadn't raised me to be quite so tolerant, polite and patient. My carpenter has suggested drastic measures, but I keep on calling the same number and leaving a message. Wish I could think of someway to impress upon them that the sound of drip-drip-drip annoys me.

There are only four roofing companies in town. Looks as if I chose the wrong one. I've decided to suggest to them that they change their slogan. They certainly aren't keeping *me* dry.

Oh well, think positive. It does cause me to look forward to winter. I'm hoping snow will fall soon so the leaks will cease.

A friend tells me, "Looks as if the only solution for you is to keep on dabbing that patch stuff on the bad spots." That's just fine. I've been doing that for three years. I didn't mind so much before I paid to have the whole thing replaced, but who wants to hold a thumb in the dike after it's been rebuilt.

I've taken to putting house plants in the puddle places. It's a little bit messy when the drips splash in the dirt, but at least I'm not wasting the water.

> Love from your dampish daughter,
> Dee

OFF THEY GO AGAIN

Dear Sharron and Will,

It's the end of August, the end of summer, the end of vacation and a cold, wet, blustery day. Since I ought to be doing something constructive, I think I'll sit here and feel sorry for myself.

School is about to begin. Blek! I always think of you two when it's time to send the children off to school. I know you also resent having to part with your favorite people for so much of each day so much of the year.

All summer long, every single day, I have enjoyed the barefooted, bike-riding bustling about; the schemes and dreams and observations; the energy and enthusiasm of my three spirited offspring. Now I've got to relinquish them to regimentation in the interest of education. Another September trauma. Only difference is, this year it occurs in August.

How well I remember that first painful separation. Young Son was in the stroller. I held Middle Child firmly by the hand. We marched into the schoolyard behind our perky little kindergartener, The Eldest. Off she ran to the swings with not so much as a glance over her shoulder.

Anticipating tears from some less bold newcomers, I asked the teacher, Mrs. Rajander, about the plan of action in case of tantrums. (I had been designated room mother and assigned to serve coffee and donuts to the mothers after the bell rang.)

"Oh, I never have any trouble with the children," she assured me, "only with the mothers. Distracting them is your job." I think the job had fallen to me because the P.T.A. president, a good friend and neighbor, realized that the mother most likely to have trouble adjusting was bound to be me.

As predicted, once the bell rang, the mothers stood with noses pressed to the window peering with great anguish at all those eager little faces which had so obviously forgotten us forever.

"They're so little." "So cute." "They look so happy." We

sniffed forlornly, watching as the condemned submitted to storytime.

All 32. . . . Wait a minute! 33!? Mrs. Rajander wasn't quite right. This first day wasn't going to go off without a hitch after all. There at one inconspicuous edge of the cluster of alert and attentive little learners sat a tiny toddler, calmly sucking her thumb. Oblivious to everything, including instructions to scoot out into a circle, Middle Child was pleased as punch to suddenly find herself literally the center of attention.

There were subdued giggles and expressions of glee from classmates, but no inappropriate behavior, as the big sister whispered and gestured and the little one solidly shook her head. NO! Torn between tears and laughter, I tiptoed in to remove the stowaway. I had indeed succeeded in providing a bit of diversion for the mothers.

A few nights ago the stowaway finally developed some apprehension about school, eleven years late. I overheard her say, "High school's going to be awfully big and scary, Lia. Would you mind showing me around the first day?"

"Don't worry, Jill. You'll do just fine. Stick with me until you feel comfortable," was the sympathetic reply.

How come nobody sticks with me so that the first day doesn't seem so empty each year?

Condolences,
Dee

HAPPY HOLIDAY

September 5, 1978

Dear Sis,

Labor Day. Pushing a pencil does not qualify as an acceptable Alaskan activity on this day of humble homage to honest effort, but I'm too weary and sore to move anything heavier at this hour. In fact, I've chosen a very small pencil.

Labor Day. I can just imagine how *you* spent this day. It is blasphemous how lowlanders so irreverently desecrate, I mean celebrate, this holiday. On a day set aside for special recognition of the working person I'll just bet you went waterskiing, lay basking in the sun or sipped lemonade by the side of a pool somewhere. That's disgusting. I'm not jealous. I'm zealous.

Labor Day is an important day for Alaskans. We have reason to appreciate the significance of this event. It is a solemn occasion to be treasured. It is the one chance (with any luck) we have to safely and comfortably do all the things that should be done before the snow flies.

We can (and I did) wash the windows inside and out without having to worry about soapy water freezing to the glass.

We can (and I did) put large bulky items like the wheelbarrow somewhere specific so that though we can't get to them all winter we will at least know where to expect them to surface in the spring.

We can (and I did) break up brush piles for kindling; attack the long wood with a chain saw and stack cord wood—the better to find it when the cold comes (next week).

We can (and I did) dig potatoes, pull carrots and freeze the brussel sprouts.

We can (and I did) search through storage areas to find snow tires, chains, the meat grinder, parkas, long underwear, mitten making knitting needles and 42 jars for canning green tomatoes.

We can (but Young Son and his father wouldn't let me come along) be tramping over muskeg and tussocks with umpteen pounds of bloody moose meat dripping down our backs.

We could (if we had water) empty and store the hoses. (Skipping that chore was something of a mixed blessing.)

We can (but I didn't) staple visqueen over windows and weather stripping around doors without risking injury from frostbitten fingers and ears.

We can (and still I didn't) do all the things that we should have done during the summer to keep us warm and snug for the winter.

We can (briefly) get organized. I didn't.

Everywhere else this day signals the end of summer fun. Here it heralds sensible preparation for winter so that we can enjoy our ever so swift, brief, crisp fall.

After all the chores are done. We can (and I did) get together with splendid friends for fun, frolic, good food, games and dancing.

I'm trying to convince myself it was the chain saw and not the volleyball that caused the soreness and fatigue. Guess I won't really know until I test the muscles and see whether reaching up or down hurts more.

Don't you wish you had something significant to do to appropriately squander this day upon? I'm glad it only comes once a year. I don't have the energy to celebrate it more often.

Big Sis

HOW OLD ARE YOU?

September 11, 1978

Dear Sis,

Just discovered something that I've had tucked away since the kids were little. It's my version of a little guy explaining the answers he received to a question he had asked of various people. Believe that little guy is in college now.

> I asked my grandma,
>> How old are you?
> And she said,
>> Old, old, old.
> I asked Aunt Janice,
>> How old are you?
> And she said,
>> Over twenty-one.
> I asked Aunt Alice,
>> How old are you?
> And she said,
>> Never ask a lady!

I asked Mrs. Tobias,
>How old are you?

And she said,
>The very idea!

I asked my grandpa,
>How old are you?

And he said,
>Old as the hills.

I asked Uncle Dalton,
>How old are you?

And he said,
>Much too old.

I asked my mommy,
>How old are you?

And she said,
>Younger than I feel.

I asked Bobby,
>How old are you?

And he said,
>Five years old.
>>Why?

Because I asked a lot of grown-ups
>And none of them knew.

I'm five years old too.
>Maybe you forget when you get older.

How often do you suppose we dismiss an honest inquiry from our kids, or anyone for that matter with a frivolous or flippant answer that confuses rather than communicates?

All this cogitating came about because on a glum day too many people asked me, "How you doing?," and I told them. Each time I answered I'd get a surprised look as if I hadn't answered correctly. If they didn't really want to know, why did they ask me in the first place?

How are you, Sis? I really, really want to know. Write me a letter and tell me the truth.

>Much love and I miss you,
>Sis

GROWING HOME

September 18, 1978

Dear Sharron and Will,

It's certainly been a long time since I've heard from you, but then it's been a long time since I've written too. When we first moved up here, my nearest neighbor was also a newcomer and she was desperately homesick.

All she could talk about was the neighborhood she left behind, the house she had to relinquish, the furniture they couldn't ship and friends and relatives back home who were all within a day's driving distance of each other. She spent much money and time on the phone planning a trip "home" for as soon as it could possibly be arranged.

The neighborhood we left behind was crowded and unfriendly, the house wasn't ours and we didn't own any furniture. I did miss friends and relations, but our budget didn't allow phone calls. I wrote page after page of glowing prose about the wonders of this paradise we'd discovered.

My intention was to lure everyone we cared about north. That way we wouldn't miss them and they wouldn't miss partaking of this incredible world of scenic delights, wide open spaces and warm, friendly people.

One day I mentioned my mushy correspondence to a good friend and longtime Alaskan resident. "The trouble is," I said with a frown, "I don't think the folks down there actually believe me when I tell them how great it is up here."

His outburst startled me. "Edee, stop it! Don't tell people what it's *really* like up here. This place is crowded enough as it is. Tell them the last ship north was the one you came up on and the road's been washed out. Tell them it's miserable, horrible and you hate it. Tell them the only reason you aren't returning immediately is that it's a financial disaster and you simply can't afford to leave. Tell them ice fog is toxic, mosquitoes carry malaria and cabin fever is fatal, but don't tell them the truth!"

In spite of his fervor it took me several years to get over trying to entice everyone I cared about to join us in our chosen land. The change occurred gradually. I don't mean that I became less enamored of the people, the place or the

129

possibilities. I just got too engrossed in enjoying life to proselytize.

Letters (or phone calls) started out as a desperate need flowing fast in both directions, then slowed to a steady exchange important for keeping in touch, dwindled to a sporadic note here and there and now are a nagging "should" that rarely ever fits into a busy schedule.

I don't miss "home" less. This just gradually has become home. Roots grow. Memories accumulate. Friendships deepen. Commitments emerge. People, places and parts of life weave into a pattern that fits. Alaskans do tend to believe that no one has it as good as we do. Which is a nice outlook considering the disadvantages we have to put up with, but deep down in my heart I realize that the reason you are too busy to write is exactly the same. We're all enthusiastically involved in enjoying life and no matter where you are that's a nice place to be.

I'm still sorry that you're not up here with me or I'm not down there with you, but isn't it splendid that we are all so happy with where we are! However, just in case you might change your mind, why don't you come up and take a look around.

Dee

BLOODY REVENGE

September 25, 1978

Dear Mom and Dad,

I haven't told you about the moose yet! Goodness me! It's been ages. (Well, not all *that* long.), but a couple of weeks anyway, since Young Son and his father brought home the beast.

They left, just like always, the night before the season opened in "their" area; were gone, just like always, a bit over a week; and came back, just like always, with a vehicle full of entrees waiting to be discovered. Just like that.

130

This year they walked in rather than being flown in and this year friends and neighbors warned me not to get my hopes up because "it's too warm" and "it's too early" and "nobody's gotten a moose for several years."

Well, it might have been too early for the moose, but it was just right for us. I've tried to entertain people, whose fall-long reluctant refusals consisted of, "Well, we'd really love to, but don't count on us. We just can't plan anything until after we've gotten our moose." This crew always gets the hunt and the slaughter over with immediately so we can relax and enjoy the crisp, quick fall.

When people ask Young Son, "Who shot it?" His reply is, "I missed." It doesn't seem to occur to the boy that he isn't exactly answering the question. He forgot to release the safety before pulling the trigger and was only offered a sportsman's chance. (Just like Dad never *letting* me win at chess.)

The butchering this year was really great! Always before there have been too many experts. As an amateur my lot has been to have formless blobs tossed my direction along with commands like: Thud. "Label T-Bones." Thud. "Pot Roast." Thud. "Stew." "Kghh." "Beg your pardon?" "*I was just clearing my throat.*" "oh." Tense silence.

Dully I cut the paper, plopped blobs, folded, taped, labeled, stacked and plodded about like a drone.

This year was splendid! I was given my very own hind end to dissect. Middle Child was given a full front end. Then to top it off the instructors left us alone with our prizes. If you've ever heard a cat growl as it hovers over a choice morsel you've only a gentle idea of our intensity.

We sculpted muscles, defined tendons, excercised the old boy to see what moved when he walked and searched for familiar cuts like eye-of-the-round and cross-rib roasts. (Never did find one of those.) We poked our fingers in to see what was tough and what was tender and did such a thorough job that all we ended up with was two long white shiny clean jointed pieces of what looked like a museum skeleton.

The frustration of packaging slipped my mind entirely until I went to fix dinner tonight. There are various ways of getting even in this world and I guess if you tell your assistant to quit complaining and keep wrapping you should expect job dissatisfaction to crop up in whatever way it may.

I just discovered we now have a freezer full of carefully chosen cuts of meat all wrapped appropriately in crisp white paper and labeled in a firm, if belligerent hand with such outbursts as: "An Incredible Hulk," "Organic Protein," "Barbariously Butchered Beast" and "What You See Is What You Get."

Next year I'm going to suggest a more equal division of labor.

Love,
Dee

PONY EXPRESS

October 2, 1978

Dear Sis,

Have you seen that little sign of mine that says, "I don't care what the whole world knows about me as long as my mother never finds out?" Mom thinks it's terribly funny. I want to find one for her that says, "When communicating by mail, explain everything to your daughter except what you're talking about."

She reminds me of the mother who gave a full blown explanation of the birds and bees to the kid who asked where he came from (The appropriate answer was Chicago.).

Really, I shouldn't complain. There's nothing I hate more than an empty mail box. I've tried to get my local post office persons to put a note in my box to comfort me when there isn't any mail, but they consider that above and beyond the call of duty.

There's no getting around it, communicating by mail can be confusing and frustrating. Incidentally, could you do me a favor and find out if all of our relatives are alive and well? I just received four carefully penned pages from Mother about some disaster which has befallen "your aunt and uncle" but there is no mention of *what* happened or which of our 17 aunts and uncles she is referring to.

132

Reminds me of the time Chris was thrown from a horse. Mom wrote, described the traumatic scene, reassured me that though both wrists were sprained and there were "some other injuries" Chris was doing nicely. I was definitely not to worry a bit. She went on about the weather and such and then closed by saying, "Really must go. Ron is teasing Chris because she can't walk. I have to go help move her. Love, Mom."

It only took me two letters and three weeks to learn that what kept Chris from walking was stiffness and sore muscles, not that she was crippled permanently.

Mom has another frustrating habit which I really suspect is her way of seeing if I'm paying attention. She alludes to some great morsel of gossip or bit of drama and then says, "but, of course, I've told you about that already." The man standing next to me in the post office last week jumped six inches and apologized profusely when I shouted in his ear, "Oh, NO! you haven't."

Mom has a method for speeding up correspondence which she calls positive thinking. Her letter begins, "I'm just certain that if I write this now I will get a letter from you in today's mail." (I'm just as certain as I read it that she won't because I haven't written for several weeks.) She must go out and weed the garden after that because the next line reads, "The mail box was empty, but I know that I will hear from you tomorrow." The only certainty about tomorrow is that I *might* get around to writing.

Sitting down and putting pen to paper takes so much time. I'd really rather call her, but I hate to pay to hear her say, "You must get off the phone, this is costing you money." She could send me a telegram with more words in it than I get out of her over the phone.

I've got a new plan though. Next time I write a long letter I'm going to send it to her a page at a time. If she reads letters like she writes them I figure she'll never even notice. Must sign off, but do me a favor, please, phone Mom and tell her I'll write soon.

Love,
Sis

GONE WITH THE WIND

Dear Mom and Dad,

I said that I would describe to you our magnificent fall, but I've waited too long. It's all over now. It ended with surprising abruptness the weekend that September gave way to October. The last of the leaves fell, the temperature dropped and snow began drifting down out of the clouds. Nicely enough my spirits rose at about the same time so I've energy available to belatedly describe the sumptuous season.

Fall is usually our one gradual transition. Spring green seems to burst upon us when we turn our heads. Snow and cold can appear overnight. Summer is too often one brief hot month in July. Fall, however, takes pleasure in unfolding at a leisurely pace while watching people bustle about preoccupied with winterizing cars, spreading plastic over windows, hunting food, gathering wood, securing water systems and generally scurrying like squirrels.

Finally finished with autumnal activities, we settle back to appreciate the splendid scenery and what we see is, the leaves have disappeared, the trees are bare. We missed it.

Fall is a sensual season, ushered in by the chattering of geese overhead and an overwhelming odor. The smell is sticky, thick, and musty—so bad it's good, or so good it's bad. You can't quite tell. The density would be understandable pervading a stuffy room, but this sensation is thick enough to slice and serve with ice cream and it goes roaming all over the countryside. The flavor is highbush cranberries, one day spiced with warm dust, the next with damp dirt and wet leaves.

Fall actually does offer mouth-watering taste treats: the last of the fresh vegetables, berries that haven't been frozen, still bloody moose meat, smoked salmon, coleslaw and beer so cold it hurts to hold it in spite of a mitten and a bonfire.

Chain saws roar and buck and nag as they attack winter wood supplies throughout the neighborhood. Hammers and saws echo from one building project to another with an urgency

134

spurred by mittened hands. Leaves crunch underfoot and the earth begins to feel solid again.

Of course, our most precisely calibrated barometer is vegetation. All summer long we are surrounded by hillsides resplendent with lush green birch trees laced with dark spruce. One morning when fog drifts down from the north over the hill into the valley it leaves behind a bright yellow stain. The fog disperses. The color remains. Another day a new patch develops across the way.

Bit by bit green gives way to brilliant orange, red, yellow and gold. Sunshine on the hill creates an illusion of motion. At times the transition is almost tangible. Where the first yellow splash occurred a shadow falls. The leaves are gone. The pattern and texture become fur-like. From a distance the hills resemble a gigantic crouching animal.

Close at hand is fireweed, a plant that sports a tall, lovely bright purple flower in its prime. As summer dwindles its leaves turn the colors of flame and the flower becomes a smoke-like fluff of white that drifts with the wind.

Fantastic! All of it! Do we marvel at this grandeur and magnificence? A bit, but more often we remark with regret that winter is on its way. Such is the short sightedness of humans.

> Much love, wish I could
> see Bloomfield's fall,
> Dee

EMPTY SHELVES

November 6, 1978

Dear Mom and Dad,

Realize I haven't written for a long, long time. Let me explain. Note the stationery (or absence of it) from me! Your eldest daughter, who would rather go barefoot in the snow than write on anything less than elegant parchment, is paperless. We used to have a funny little crowded card shop downtown that was so inconvenient it was an adventure to visit. The stock was so plentiful that I inched around in fear of knocking things over and I always spent too much time and money there.

One day during the pipeline, this source of delightful messages and stack upon stack of charming, elegant and ever so appropriate paper-to-put-pen-to disappeared. Crass customer that I am, I didn't even mourn the passing of this little hole in the wall filled with delights for the eyes and tugs for the pocketbook.

Stationery is an easy thing for me to squander cash upon. Such a bargain! In each box are 15, 20, maybe even 25 lovely presents for friends and family members whose days will be immensely brightened by the texture, quality, design, color and message. You get the picture.

I didn't think much about the loss of my source of stationery because at the same time in two very convenient locations two very large card shops appeared. Obviously my horizons were about to be broadened by more and better kinds of stationery. Right? WRONG!

In this case, more is less. What you have been receiving of late has been the very last of my hoarded odds and ends: a special last sheet that I didn't want to part with (plain typing paper behind it); a note card I'd really hoped to frame (sacrificed to the drought); a postcard from our trip to Mexico two years ago and so forth.

For months and months and months the shelves of both of these large, convenient shops have been empty. The first few weeks I chalked it up to late stock. We have a lot of that up here. After a month or so (I can be a very patient woman) I began making comments such as: "Do you intend to go out of business?" "Are you trying to encourage customers to go elsewhere?" And so forth.

Gradually my agitation has escalated and at this point my children will not allow me to go near either store. When we are in the area the largest child distracts me while one of the others checks the inventory. Then they gently suggest our shopping trip is over, insisting we really must get home before the ice cream melts.

I know they are protecting me from myself. Their plan is transparent. For one thing the freezer is full of moose, halibut, berries and salmon and we haven't been able to buy ice cream for over a month. For another thing, the car heater isn't working and nothing ever melts in that car.

I have considered such violent retribution against those places of business that it scares me, but none so drastic as my present plan. This morning when I reached for a piece of pretty paper upon which to write this letter to you there was absolutely, positively nothing there but a red plastic swizzle stick and a broken pencil with no eraser.

This morning I vowed never again to use stationery. I will buy new mukluks with the money I save. From a dusty old box stored under the stairs I have unearthed a lifetime supple of letter writing material. Stationery stores be damned!

That is why this letter to you is written on the back of a lab sheet from Zoology 101. I suspect those funny splotches are frog guts, but this piece was in much better condition than the mutilated notes from Chemistry 1A. You, my dear parents, are about to experience the true value of a college education.

Much love,
Dee

EUREKA!

Dear Sis,

Do you remember when we were kids that Mom would gleefully announce, "I've found it!!" when she reached the last piece in the ironing basket? Part of the game was to ask eagerly *what* she had found. Then she would go on about how the *last* piece was the very piece she had been looking for all along.

Well, my accomplishment is bound to be about as short-lived as an empty ironing basket, but finally "I've found it!"

For over a year now I've been pouring every bit of time, energy, money, anxiety and anticipation into this house to try to civilize it enough so that it feels inhabitable.

First of all, I thought that having a custon-built kitchen with painted walls, cabinets and a counter top would make me feel as if I lived in a real house. No, the contrast between finished and un- just made the livingroom's soggy ceiling more obvious and odious.

The vicious circle was set in motion. A covered ceiling caused the log walls to cry out to be sanded and varathaned. Once I'd spiffied up those I found myself desperate for the built-in couch I'd dreamed of for so long.

When that accomplishment didn't satisfy the now obsessive nesting urge I began looking in earnest for the crowning glory. I trimmed the kitchen with Mexican tile. The rest of the family declared the effect magnificent. I just noticed cracks in the grout. I painted floors. I commissioned construction of a sophisticated bedroom closet complete with doors that open and close, but still I wanted more. The search seemed endless, until. . . .

I found it! I am happy to announce that though there are still two rooms without wall-covering; many places where sheetrock has yet to be taped let alone painted; floors that are bare and ugly; ceilings that badly need attention; and running water is only a distant dream—I have found the piece I was looking for.

It's so obvious that I wonder why I didn't discover it before. I have just acquired a corner stone that exudes stability, security, longevity and an overall aura of having arrived. Placed prominently in the dominant area of our livingroom, squarely under the much-cherished and nurtured heat source I now have a solid stone hearth of quite substancial dimensions.

It's useless to tell you the actual dimensions. The livingroom is 7 or 8 sided, depending upon whether or not you count a narrow open spot as a wall. The perimeter of the hearth, like the room itself, has angles that have angles. Just let me say that at the widest point the hearth is 4 1/2' x 10' and 5'' thick.

The justification for investing in this extravagant slab of stone and mortar was safety, but I'm well aware of the fact that there would have been cheaper, simpler and less massive means of managing the problem. However, for a woman whose aesthetic sense is grounded largely in appreciation of permanence, functionality, sturdiness, strength and size, this is the Taj Mahal.

So here I sit on my built-in couch, surrounded by sanded walls and all appreciating my lovely livingroom? Of course not! I'm busy designing shelves and wood storage for the wall across from me. No one ever expected the ironing basket to *remain* empty.

Just,
Sis,

SWIFT SEASONAL SHIFTS

November 20, 1978

Dear Mom and Dad,

Yes, we have snow *already*. We've had it for a month and ten days. It seems just as strange to me for you to be raking leaves as it does to you for me to be shoveling snow.

The day of the first real snow this year impressed me because it was sudden, dramatic, thorough, complete and on my birthday. Early in the day I gazed out a window and commented that the crisp, clear fall weather was a birthday bonus too good to be true. I should have kept my mouth shut.

Three busy hours later I gasped in astonishment when what to my wondering eyes did appear but a blanket of snow covering everything everywhere and a blur in the air as the stuff continued to fall out of the sky. That sort of drama is supposed to happen overnight to give the impression Jack Frost did it, but instead, in broad daylight the wonder of winter was arriving.

"Oh, isn't it lovely!" "We'll be skiing soon!" And other exclamations of appreciation ended abruptly when we tried to go home. Just because the onslaught was overdue, do not assume that we were ready. Too many of us were caught without our snow tires, winter driving sense, chains, handy man jack, and sand or gravel in the rear (dual purpose dirt for sprinkling and ballast).

If you speeded up you fishtailed. If you slowed down you had trouble moving at all. Once you were moving, prayers seemed more efficient than brakes. It was scary. I aged more than a year that day. Cars punctuated the ditches. Collisions complicated the traffic. People had to wait in line for tow trucks and I needed my studded tires.

Once I safely reached home I heaved a sigh of relief, loaded studded tires into the car, gathered my courage and prepared to hurry off (slowly) to my nearby friendly, reliable service station. On second thought, I called first. An unfamiliar voice insisted "No. Not now. Probably not even tomorrow, but we could try."

(So should I "try" to drive 36 miles to work tomorrow in these conditions with no snow tires?)

"Oh, Mom! What will you do?" my sympathetic crew exclaimed.

"Well, first of all, I'll appear in person. If that doesn't work, I can always explain that it's my birthday. (Though I doubt they'll believe me.) The big accomplishment is going to be to get there safely. Whatever you kids do—Don't worry about me."

Off I slid. Somehow I arrived safely at my destination. I walked into the station, straight to my efficient and understanding mechanic. I didn't even have a chance to utter my well-rehearsed plea. Before I could open my mouth, Greg said, "Edee, you don't have your snow tires on!"

I nodded grimly.

"You haven't hit anyone have you?" He asked anxiously.
"Not yet."

"Pull your car into the first bay and let's get that taken care of right away!" He commanded.

OH! the warmth and comfort of someone who cares in a cold, cruel world. Thank heaven some of the angels of mercy were placed in sensible places like service stations.

Now the major threat the snow holds is that it keeps covering up the wood pile. Happy leaf raking. Sorry we won't be able to go over the river and through the woods for Thanksgiving, but we'll be thinking of you.

Your loving daughter,
Edith C.

HOLIDAY ADAPTATIONS

November 27, 1978

Dear Sis,

How was your Thanksgiving? Did you all go over the river and through the woods to visit Mom and Dad or did they come down out of the hills to dine in the suburbs? When Grandma lived on the farm I used to feel *so* privileged to travel off to a truly *Saturday Evening Post* celebration.

My most vivid childhood recollection of turkey day is the year I sat fidgeting with the tablecloth while grown-ups talked interminably. I ruined the lace edge in front of me and they had no trouble tracking down the villian. How humiliating! I was old enough to know better, but too young to sit still.

Holidays are one time when it feels quite strange to be up here so far from the family, but when it comes to celebrations we're far from underprivileged.

Surely the most treasured holiday for our three will always be Halloween. Sub-zero temperatures and houses many acres apart aren't exactly conducive to trick or treat so the locals have adapted to the climate. Talk about tradition! The annual "neighborhood" event is older than any of the kids who compete for crashing the piñata. Guests of all ages wear costumes so elaborate we can't recognize each other. Each year includes a gigantic bonfire, tasty pot luck, apple bobbing, sauna, sledding, dancing and volleyball in the snow and buff.

For our first Fairbanks Thanksgiving, we were invited to join several families who hadn't seen their own kinfolk for ages. They have created a pattern of holiday celebration over the years that embraces those who choose to be together instead of those who were born to share the same table.

We cross-country skied during the daylight at a brisk -6 degrees. My California background kept me marveling at our mere survival. Not only were we able to breathe and move about, the exertion made it necessary to stop and "cool off" by exposing some bit of flesh to the elements.

As if she suspected homesickness might be lurking in the corners of our hearts, our hostess (Judy, as you might suspect) kept us happy, distracted and superbly fed. After dinner and dishes the adults were sprawled Roman fashion about the rug basking in the glow of the fire, thankful that they need not move, when some of the sledders (all under age) burst upon us. They wanted company for their exhilaration. So sled we did.

That was a year of superfluous snow and after the sledding the small boys and some not so small competed to see who could do the most ridiculous stunts by diving into the snow from the highest points available. The less hardy drifted indoors alternately watching through windows and standing with backs to the fire.

Suddenly a small messenger from the out of doors burst in to announce that all the children had been buried and could not be found! We toasty ones were beseeched to rush out to the rescue. Half-heartedly we stood on the deck above and oohed and ahed and joked about the disappearance of our loved ones. The real joke was that the children refused to emerge on cue and the fathers became truly worried about their wicked deed.

There was such general hilarity when at last the little people emerged in triumph. They had fooled *everyone*! What a much nicer diversion than toying with the edge of a lace table cloth.

Happy, happy holidays from your only a wee bit homesick sister.

Dee

TOURING TOWN

December 4, 1978

Dear Auntie Carolyn,

I've just discovered an adventure in my own town. I highly recommend it. You could try it down there too. In fact, it can be done most anywhere. I've done it in Mexico City; Vancouver, B.C.; Guaymas, Mexico; San Francisco and Los Angeles, but I never thought about doing it in Fairbanks, Alaska.

The adventure was forced upon me. My car has a crush on my mechanic and just as soon as I get one bill paid off the vehicle develops a new reason to spend the day with good company in the warmth of the shop.

I can't complain much. This time it chose moderate weather and a convenient time to demand attention, but it did leave me with one substantial problem, a need to get to work in two different parts of town and no cab fare in my pocket. I started out to walk (I don't hitch hike), but that would have taken ever so long and my toes got cold.

So I took the bus. That was my adventure. For 50¢ I settled back in a warm, comfortable, pleasant couch and explored parts of my town that I never knew existed. It was delightful! The driver was excellent. For part of the trip I amused myself by marveling at his expertise. After herding one of those mechanical giants 11,000 miles from here to Guaymas and back with the Alaska Highway thrown in for good measure my admiration for bus drivers is limitless.

There I sat, comfy-cozy, up in the air, able to look out and not required to pay attention to where we were going. Such luxury! There was so much to see that I steamed up the window gawking at a town I'd never noticed before.

Being a passenger on a bus brought back so many childhood memories. I used to make up lives for the strangers when I was little. I used to try to read their minds and loved eavesdropping on conversations. Inevitably in those days I ended up spending my bus fare home and put myself in a terrible predicament. I almost did the same thing (at my age!) again. I forgot that I was carless and was tempted to buy an apple fritter to go with my coffee.

Bus drivers still seem to be the same extra nice guys that they always were so I suspect they might have allowed me to "owe" it to them just as they did in the olden days, but I didn't have the courage to try. (I always paid them back.)

The buses I met were so on time it was a marvel. I wonder why more people don't ride the bus? The combined cab fare for my adventure would have been $9.00 plus tax for a dull direct route. The fare on the bus for the various rides was $1.50 and the round-about route we traveled could definitely be considered a scenic tour.

If you don't ever need to ride the bus for practical purposes, I suggest a trip as a means of offering a bright new outlook on your town and its people. Such inexpensive entertainment!

In a practical vein, in our tortuous climate, what a joy it would be to be able to give over the headaches of winter driving and vehicle maintenance to someone else. Unfortunately it is difficult to take advantage of both worlds. It isn't easy to live in the woods 36 miles from work and also leave the driving to the bus.

How I wish it were!

Greetings from your loving niece,
Edith C.

TAKE TWO ASPIRIN,
GRIN AND BEAR IT

December 11, 1978

Dear Sis,

Time may fly when you're having fun, but it sure creeps by when you stay home from work because you're really sick. On my first job that included paid sick leave, I used one day. One was enough.

The kids were little then. After an all-night siege with the flu, up and running at frequent intervals. . . . (You know the general logistics of a good case of the flu. I don't have to go into the gory details.) The next morning, after I'd fixed lunches and breakfasts and sent the family off to school, I decided I was too weak to go to work.

I called in sick, feeling very guilty. Mother's aren't supposed to get sick. I worried that those in the office wouldn't believe I was ill. (What they didn't believe was that I was dumb enough to stay home.)

As I turned from the phone, prepared to collapse into bed for a day of rest and recuperation, I was confronted with dishes piled high on all available surfaces. Since I couldn't go back to bed with the kitchen in such a mess I pulled my aching body upright and attacked the task at hand.

As a natural aspect of dispatching the dishes I cleaned the stove and refrigerator. In a fevered fog I washed and waxed the kitched floor to which I was tired of sticking. On the way to the bedroom, at last, I realized the sparkly kitchen put the rest of the house to shame so I vacuumed, dusted, picked up, did the laundry and caught up on the ironing and mending. (I could close the closet door for the first time since I started to work.)

After I'd cleaned the bathroom I assumed the house would allow my conscience and body to rest. In a freshly made bed! ? Never! I was leaning against the counter mechanically making cookies when the children burst through the door. "Hey! Mom's home! Neat! Can we go to town to buy new tennis shoes?"

In my weakened condition, how could I resist such appreciation? I nodded automatically as I watched through bleary eyes the crud being tracked across clean floors.

I learned my lesson well. The next time I was deathly ill, I eased myself silently out of bed a little early and snuck off to work. All day long I sat at my desk in stillness and quiet staring at piles of work that would just have to wait until I was feeling better. From superiors, co-workers and clients I received tea and sympathy. Not one woman asked me why I didn't stay home since I felt so lousey.

Happily I report that today I have been too incapacitated to do *anything* with my paid solitude, but watch it tick by. I don't know what I've got, but it's certainly winning.

At some point this morning I stumbled from my bed to discover I was capable of standing on my feet (a bit shaky, but almost upright). "I should have gone to work," I thought guiltily. (An interesting observation, obviously of a feverish mind, since I've lost my voice and my job consists of 8 hours of oral communication.)

As for the family, the kids tip-toed in after school, asked after my health, fed the fire, fixed themselves dinner and went quietly up to their rooms. There are some definite advantages to having teenagers.

In a whisper,
Big Sis

GOING WITHOUT

December 18, 1978

Dear Sis,

The only reason you don't understand about outages is that *you* live down where there *are* things. Up here even grocery shopping is an adventure. You never know for sure what you are going to buy until you get to the store and find out what they have. My first attempt to purchase the ingredients for a respectable company meal was an initiation. I made the mistake of deciding in advance what I thought I was going to serve. According to my usual pattern I drew up a lengthy and complete list of necessary items. Bad planning. Up here flexibility is a virtue, indecision a survival tactic.

It was a simple error, I had my entire menu structured around a sumptuous recipe for Mexican Leg of Lamb. At that time, as near as I can figure out, someone somewhere in Muttonville had convinced the shippers, packers and transporters of the world that Fairbanksans don't eat lamb. There wasn't even one moldy chop in this entire town. I went home, took out my cookbooks and started all over again.

Such is the plight of the isolated housewife. You get used to it after a few years. There is a plot afoot, again, to wean us from wooden matches. It's happened before. In a land where candles and kerosene are essential (due to power outages), where woodheat is a common source of comfort and propane a clever fuel for cooking it will soon be necessary to buy and discard a pack of cigarettes in order to get matches. Smokers are going to have to give up their nasty habit just to keep warm and cook dinner.

As long as we're on the subject of doing without, do you know if cream of tartar is still produced? After several seasons without snickerdoodles or angel food cakes I just marked it out of the recipes. If Ralph Nader ever discovers it's bad for your health Alaskans can take comfort in the fact that they gave it up years ago.

Once we had a yo-yo scarcity. The explanation: "It isn't the time of year for yo-yos." Now I can see a time of year for straw hats, mittens, candy canes and mosquito repellant (all of which are on the shelves year-round) but what decides which time of year is right for yo-yos?

At times I'm philosophical—you can't have everything. (In fact, at times it seems as if you can't have anything.) Then it gets to me. I feel manipulated. I begin to imagine a person somewhere "down below" crouched over a large planning board, chuckling sinisterly and cackling, "Next we will do away with blondes in Alaska. Henceforth no hair product calculated to lighten, brighten or highlight hair shall be sent to 99701. Just to be safe, scratch hydrogen peroxide too. They can use methiolate for skinned knees."

Call us paranoid if you like, but it is a known and demonstrable fact that in Notown, U.S.A., when a product has sat upon the shelves for over a generation or two they say, "Send it back to the distributor so that they can ship it to Alaska."

Don't tell me I'm feeling sorry for myself. I'm tough. I can prove it. I've done without paprika for 21 months, improvised toilet paper for weeks at a time, given up coffee filters for my particular funnel, survived suetless for an entire moose season, and consoled countless kindergarteners who were deprived of finger painting due to a dearth of liquid starch. Why I. . . .

Oh, dear me! Sis, upon re-reading this letter, I find I've been unnecessarily harsh and negative. I do apologize. Christmas shopping must be getting to me. My main reason for writing was to wish you a MERRY, MERRY CHRISTMAS and all the joys of the season.

Ho, Ho, Ho,
Big Sis

DAILY NEWS-MINER,
Fairbanks, Alaska
   Wednesday, Dec. 27, 1978

LETTERS TO THE EDITOR
Thanks for Edee

December 18, 1978

Dear Editor,
   Every Monday evening I come home from work and read Edee Rohde's letter from Alaska and say to myself, "Tomorrow I'm going to write a letter to the editor saying how much I like them." The problem is that it is difficult for me to say how much I enjoy them without gushing.

   So often I recognize my own experiences. Once in awhile there's ever a tear or two. Anyway, thank you, Editor, for giving me Edee Rohde's letter's. Thank you, Edee, for saying things so well.

Sincerely,
Judy Mimken

THANK YOU TOO!

January 8, 1979

Dear Whole Buncha People,

My thanksgiving time always comes at the *end* of the holiday season, rather than the beginning. For me November's Thanksgiving is a feast day, a fun get together time, the beginning of the end of the year. I bustle about the kitchen all day long, feeling like the olden days.

My hands are busy preparing edibles. My mind is busy organizing Christmas preparations to begin at dawn the next day. (Though dawn is no big deal in Alaska in November.) Inevitably I forget about being thankful.

The month that follows is always happy, but hectic and filled far too full for reflection. Once the holidays are over, the New Year has begun (and I have recuperated), I pause, relax, look back on the season, on the year, on many years and get peaceful, pleased and appreciative.

This tendency to be grateful could be attributed to my upbringing and the emphatic importance placed on "thank you" and thank you letters, but whatever causes the inclination, I'm thankful for my thankfulness and for so many other things.

I'm thankful for innumerable relationships with people who are caring, understanding and accepting. It seems to me that I've more than my share of friends, relatives and acquaintances who rally round at sad times, rejoice with me at glad times, and accept me just the way I am in spite of obvious multiple imperfections. That's nice.

I could admit to being exceedingly thankful for the good fortune of being the mother of three terrific kids, but that might seem a bit boastful so I'll only consider that blessing privately.

I'm thankful to be at home in a land where living life on my own terms is possible, allowed, accepted and even encouraged by the environment and the attitude of the people.

I'm thankful that in all seasons I'm surrounded by beauty just waiting to be noticed and I don't have to go elsewhere to see spectacular mountains, hills, trees, rivers or the sky. I like that.

I'm thankful to be in an area where there is enough distance between individuals that strangers can be kind to each other and smile when they interact.

I'm thankful for a challenging, satisfying job that entails working with fascinating people, big and small, and to be exploring a little bit of talent that as a kid I dreamed would be my destiny.

Life has been good to me. I've loved a lot and learned a lot and had a lot of fun along the way.

This year has brought us good health with only one broken leg, a few sniffles and a flu or two. We've all been able to stretch and grow individually and in relation to each other. And, finally, after all these years, I'm thankful to be me. That's a welcome feeling.

I'm thankful too for you, Judy Mimken, and for all the others who read my mail and relish life in this best of all possible worlds.

Lets' hope that 1979 brings each and everyone of us much to be thankful for.

Most sincerely,
Edee Rohde

THE BLAHS

January 15, 1979

Dear Somebody!

Help! I think I'm suffering from darkness. Why is it that once we're supposed to be gaining light, dark afternoons are intolerable. The pretty pink glow in the morning grows and the middays are noticeably brighter, but the terminal aspect inevitably falls like a cement guillotine.

150

All those charts and things that indicate when the sun shall rise and set, how cold it could be, should be, was once or might be, foretell that we are inching toward summer. But none of those numbers counteract the fact that dark is dreary when it's only three o'clock in the afternoon.

For today, we have 9:27 a.m. to 2:35 p.m. which is 5 hrs. 8 mins. of daylight (big deal) a gain of 6 mins. (hardly noticeable). Abs. max. (whatever that is) was 34° in 1937 (before I was born); abs. min. was -64° in 1934 (luckily also before my natal day). Avg. max. of -3°, avg. min. of -22° and norm of -13° average out to COLD. So what do all those numbers have to do with the mid-winter blues? Don't confuse me with facts. I'm depressed.

Depression is terribly funny if you are not under the influence (of it). Somehow the gloomy are never in the right frame of mind to appreciate the humor. I've a friend named Eeyore (that's an alias) who is so gloomy that talking to he-she-or-it invaribly cheers me up.

According to this friend, January in Fairbanks, Alaska, is cold, dark, dreary, lonely, fattening and expensive. Skin dries out, stings and cracks; wood doesn't split but extension cords do; cars won't start, but furnaces never stop; house plants suffer terminal illnesses and the neighbor's dogs are ravenous and undoubtedly will break loose momentarily and eat us for lunch. (That's the picture on one of Eeyore's good days.)

At times I suggest with exaggerated enthusiasm, "Let's *do* something! We can go cross-country skiing at midday; drive up on a hill and have a picnic while we watch the sun paint the mountains pink; talk a walk through the woods and look for rabbit tracks; ride the bus across town and back; go to the library and watch the shaggy artist paint the fanciful mural; call a friend and go get. . . ."

"I'd rather complain," says Eeyore, and best no one crack a smile at the frankness of that reply.

I must admit, though, I do still *hate* the man who told me we must have some down days to balance out the ups. I've since realized he was correct, but that doesn't mean I've learned to like him or to accept the wretched idea.

One of the amusing aspects of being down in the dumps is noticing negative nuances of previously positive perceptions. If you're really good at nega-think you can almost amuse yourself into a half-hearted smile by bad-rapping the good.

Try it! When you are really blue, look around and listen to your words or thoughts. The radio's playing your favorite song (with such a lot of static). That lovely tree (appears to be drooping today, probably suffering from root rot). Your splendid new "whatever" (appears to be quite worn all of a sudden). It's Friday! (but Monday's just around the corner). See! It works! Keep going. If you are down enough there is no place to go but up!

See you there,
me

144 PAGES OF ENCOURAGEMENT

January 22, 1979

Dear Sharron,

What an absolutely fantastic book! You have no idea how delighted I was to receive it. Of course, an unexpected present out of the blue is bound to be uplifting, but just standing there in the post office reading the cover was a thrill.

THE CREATIVE WOMAN'S GETTING-IT-ALL-TOGETHER AT HOME HANDBOOK, I read, Finding Time, Finding Space, On Being Superwoman, The Playpen in the Studio, Coping with the Mess, Shifting Gears, Getting Started, Coping with Deadlines, Supporting Yourself, by Jean Ray Laury.

It pleased me to be addressed as creative, but since I believe everyone is creative, I assumed the book could easily apply to anyone at all. Little did I realize how right I was until I read it. How reassuring to read quotes from women all over the country who are also struggling with questions like: How can I justify "neglecting family and home for my own deep inner need to 'do' something."

I've hot-lined the book so that it looks as if it was printed on striped paper. Now when I'm feeling uninspired, frustrated, pressured or merely wonder what prompts me to seek rejection slips I flip through the HANDBOOK to find an appropriate uplifting comment.

It's like having all those energetic, talented women at my elbow ready to say, "Keep going! Hang in there. We're all in this together. Write on!" This has got to be *the* most significant book I've received or read in simply eons! It reads like a combination marriage manual, self-growth and realization program and guide to positive thinking and childrearing.

How nice to have someone say, "I do enjoy a clean neat house and when I do get it that way, would love to spray it with something that would make it last—I hate to do over next week what I didn't even want to do this week."

"If children are to grow, parents must grow," is music to my ears as I scream, "Damn it! Turn down the stereo. I am trying to write." Then there's: "Dirty dishes and laundry are not the exclusive possessions of wives and mother. Anyone who eats from dishes has dishes to be washed." and "Don't be selfish or self-sacrificing—be willing to share the household tasks."

"The really successful mother is, after all, dispensable. She will have taught her children to become self-sufficient and independent." Salve to the guilt I feel when Young Son goes without lunch because he's too lazy to fix it himself and I'm trying to meed a deadline.

The book assures me that, "It is important to make a commitment to yourself, choose something that you want to do or learn about and poke your head out of the warmth and security of the nest and take a chance on yourself." And "Creative women, working at home, do not just 'find' time for their work—they take it. . . ."

Nicely enough it even says, "personal relationships, everyone agrees, are what life is all about. And they do take time." So I can justify taking time out from writing to tell you how much I value the book. Thank you ever so much for sharing it with me.

Must get back to the typewriter before the kids yell down, "What's for dinner, Mom?" I'd like to frame that picture of Jean Ray Laury at the typewriter at the table in that lovely cluttered kitchen.

> 'scuse the butter,
> Dee

WISDOM OF THE AGE

January 29, 1979

Dear Auntie Carolyn,

You know how you keep something around for a long, long time because it's special or important or useful and after many years it's still on the shelf or in the back of the cupboard, but you've forgotten why you kept it. You have changed. It has changed and one day its significance is lost on you.

That's how I'm beginning to feel about teenagers. Parenthood is my most favorite occupation. Children delight me—mine and others'. In fact, I wasn't a bit surprised to read in my AstroAnalyzer that as a Libra I "make an excellent parent, probably the best of all zodiacal types." And ". . . have an affinity with children that shines through parent/child relationships in many delightful ways."

So how come the child who gave the book to me said, "Here, I sure hope this helps you figure out how to get your act together." I was just beginning to think I finally *had* gotten my act together when that 14 year old's comment brought me up short.

That must be what they're for! Teenagers descend upon us at that point in life when we oldsters are getting a bit conplacent. About the time we settle down into a peaceful, confident rut, our clever, charming children become suddenly miraculously wiser than we. It is apparently their job to give us a jolt, as often and with as much voltage as possible.

For instance, last week, completely unbidden, my lanky 13 year old son took it upon himself to explain to me discretely and solemnly that the reason our female cats were behaving so crazy, yowling and squirming all over the place, is that they have *hormones*. He paused, looked at me out of the corner of his eye and asked cautiously and uncertainly if I understood what hormones are.

I confided that I was familiar with the term and made the mistake of suggesting (in the interests of science) that this substance which he had just learned about at school *might* have something to do with some of the changes going on in his own life.

"Oh, no, Mom," he answered confidently, going on to explain with utmost patience. *"Humans* don't have hormones, only animals do."

Live and learn. Although I've kept up with new math, the introduction of the metric system and various other innovations in education I wasn't aware of this particular scientific revelation. Incidentally, where does one go to get information of this nature verified? I must admit I'm really reluctant to call up a school teacher to ask if I do or do not have hormones any more. (I am absolutely certain that I did have some at one time.)

Well, anyway, given the fact that Young Son is convinced he knows all there is to know about absolutely everything, perhaps, domestic relations would improve if I simply assumed the stance of a misguided, but willing student. I do believe I'll try that just as soon as I can catch him when his mouth isn't full and he doesn't have the headphones on or isn't on the phone. I've nothing to lose but my complacency and he's already made substantial inroads into that.

> Wish me luck,
> Edee

JUST DESSERTS

Dear Jody,

No! I cannot imagine choosing to move away from the snow country. For us snow is a feature to be sought, not shunned. Of course, if you're going to plant roots in a land where winter covers a majority of the months you might as well enjoy what you can't avoid, but of all the aspects of the solid season, snow is the one we relish.

We only ever have dessert around our house when I'm feeding the family a pretty yukky dinner. (Yukky as in skimpy, third time around leftovers or liver.) Therefore I imagine Mother Nature in the midst of planning her menu of spring, summer, fall and winter frowning and saying to herself, "What can I do to balance out the cold, dreary, dark days my children must endure? What compensation can I offer them?"

"SNOW!" Snow is obviously the dessert we receive for tolerating our many months of shivering, squinting through ice fog, slipping on icy streets and trying to explain to folks "outside" why we are foolish enough to live here. Snow is the frosting on the cake, the trees and the ski slopes. Snow denies the pain of frostbitten fingers by looking ever undeniably lovely.

From the grace of its arrival as it glides gently down out of the sky to the intriguing sculptures it creates as it melts gradually away, snow offers class, beauty, sustenance, utility, recreation and conversation.

Do you realize how many things you can do with snow? (Not you in particular since you live in Southern California, but people in general. People, that is, like us who have a lot of it to play around with.)

Melt it and drink it or wash in it or simply put a pot of it on the stove and bask in the humidity. Free moisture in the air! (Guess I've never mentioned how dry it gets up here in the winter.) Build a house out of it if you're so inclined. Eat it—snow ice cream is the ultimate confection, "yellow snow" (orange juice over) is the original slush cone. Travel on it via snow machine, dog sled, cross-country skis, sled, sleigh and snow shoes. Even cars can be quite successfully driven through it and to boot it makes a gentle cushion for the occasional inevitable, but unfortunate straying from the beaten path that comes with icy streets.

Every Alaskan child can demonstrate umpteen ways to play in it from the basic ignore it and go about the usual use of swings, slides, teeter totter, tag and football to build a snow man or fort, tunnel under and hide, ski down, escape on to it as King-of-the-Mountain or even wield it as a weapon in the form of molded missles or the threat that "I'll wash your face with snow."

Snow provides insulation. (Unless that's an old husband's tale perpetrated as an excuse for not shoveling off the roof.) Its acoustic qualities are such that a walk in the snowy woods offers absolute tranquility. It provides excellent opportunities for exercise when it must be moved about. And I'm certain there are numerous uses that I've forgotten about or don't even know about yet.

It's mind boggling! What else can you think of that is useful, lovely, edible, entertaining, slimming, soothing and free! Let's hear it for SNOW!

Meanwhile, I must go shovel some so I can mail this to you.

As ever,
Edee

LIMITED VISIBILITY

February 12, 1979

Dear Mom and Dad,

I HATE IT!! I HATE IT!! I HATE IT!! I know you always taught me: "If you can't say anything nice, don't say anything at all" and as a general policy I heartily agree. I've tried and I've tried and try as I might I cannot think of one nice thing to say about ice fog.

It's just awful. It's horrible. It's scary and ugly. It smells and it causes accidents. Really, the cold isn't so bad at all. You can bundle up against it. It's invigorating, challenging, offers something to talk about and tends to draw people together.

Ice fog does too—with a crash. Driving in it is a nightmare. I stare and concentrate as hard as I can to discern every little clue as to where I am and what might be happening. I try to conjure up telltale tail lights and street lights and signals to offer guidance as to what to expect. Eventually I begin imagining things. Clumps of snow become bunnies ready to scamper across the road. Signs develop arms and wave frantically for assistance.

To insure my safety I always evaluate the conformation of the clouds ahead. A clever and attentive person can tell when the ice fog is "fresh." (As in being made right before your very windshield.)

Fresh ice fog is the very worst of all possible kinds. It camouflages an unknown menace that can only be avoided by dropping back, back, back. On a well-traveled street a cautious driver could end up going in reverse as the fool-hardy rush blindly past into the grey unknown creating more and more grey unknown.

This evening in my trusty, but frost-encrusted, pumpkin coach I groped my way home with fingers aching due to an exceedingly firm grip on the wheel, eyes protruding, I'm sure, from the sockets, stomach tied into a fear-induced knot and muscles taut in total preparation to fight or flee. When at long last I emerged from the edge of opacity into a sunlit *visible* road I wanted to weep with joy and relief. With the light came the mind-boggling realization that. . . .

We do this to ourselves! *We* produce this wretched stuff! *We* create it! *We* make it! WE, LIVING, BREATHING, CAR-DRIVING HUMAN BEINGS, *MANUFACTURE ICE FOG*!!! I rolled down my window and shouted just that out into the minus 40 degree wind as I gazed at the sea of muck under which I assumed Fairbanks still lay.

What an accomplishment. What did you do today? Well, I manufactured 72 miles of six cylinder ice fog, not to mention one early a.m. 10 minute warm-up batch, another at midday and one final significant effort before leaving work.

We have got to be crazy! Why do we do this to ourselves and each other!? If we didn't know any better I could understand it, but why would a single. . . . (Check those passengerless cars, single is accurate indeed.) Why would a single, sensible human being willingly contribute to this unhealthy, dangerous, ugly atrocity? We have simply got to *do* something to combat this wretched problem.

As my contribution to air pollution control I have decided that I am going to volunteer to stay home in front of the fire until the cold blows over. (I'll mail this to you in the spring.)

Until then,
Dee

"HOW COLD MY TOES"

February 19, 1979

Dear Sis,

How are you? I am cold. We need hold our breath no longer. Winter has finally arrived. Here at the Woodsy Rohde Wayside we are suffering accordingly.

At my desk I hover, bundled and shivering. I have donned down booties to combat the draft across the floor, long underwear, a lap robe, two shirts and a sweater, but I refuse to wear a hat indoors and cannot possibly write in mittens. Frequent trips to the fire don't help a whole lot, because I'm so encased that the warmth can't get to me once I get to it.

As a responsible adult head of the household and a realistic human being, I am extremely reluctant to admit to anyone, let alone myself, that my house is not winterized.

Have you ever seen those little gadgets that suck up antifreeze? A lot of tiny colored bouncing balls dance around inside to tell if a car is good to 30 below or 40 below or whatever. Well, I'm a conscientious automobile owner and I take good care of my vehicle. I've poured and measured, tested, drained, poured and measured again and I'm completely confident that any gadget in this town will confirm that my mighty metal monster is good to anything below that winter can offer up.

However, since the house has never kept me from going anywhere, doesn't have to be towed if it freezes and rarely causes me to be late to work, it isn't good to anything below. In fact, at zero it begins to send out emergency messages and reminders (in triplicate) of household improvements that should have been done in 1975.

This digression is prompted by the fact that since the temperature finally dropped to a respectable low for the first time in over a year the inside of our house has begun to look increasingly like the crusted-up freezer compartment of an undefrosted refrigerator.

The reasons are all perfectly clear: the ' R-value" of 6" log walls is minimal (especially where the sill sealer is missing); much of the insulation under the house is hanging down as a result of the antics of a large dog that moved on to greener pastures years ago; most of our windows are single pain (that is not a typographical error); none of them are visqueened (I wanted to make sure it was going to get cold this winter before tending to that task.); and there is an airy draft round the door which is only now being thwarted by the fact that the door keeps freezing shut.

Actually, since we cannot see out the iced-over windows to read the thermometer, I can't tell you what the actual temperature might be, but when we have to keep moving to keep warm, cannot sit near a window or wall and dare not leave our feet on the floor lest they freeze, we concede that the season we love has finally arrived.

Don't think I'm being gloomy! There is one splendid shining ray of light in this shivering situation. The Toyota is running like a top! As a neighbor of mine once said regarding the performance of cars and houses, "Don't condemn the object, Edee, it is the owner that creates the problems."

Must close, I'm getting tired of squatting on this chair.

Big Sis

WINTER LOWS

February 26, 1979

Dear Mom and Dad,

Surely it was an Alaskan who had the wisdom, foresight and clarity of thought to coin that most profound of all statements, "If something can go wrong it will." If it wasn't an Alaskan I'm absolutely certain that it was someone who had experienced difficult winters. There is no doubt about that.

Remember Grandma's story about the man whose doctor said, "Your days are numbered, my good man. I think you had better give up smoking, drinking and the ladies as well." The man frowned and asked if he would then live longer. "Not actually," the doctor answered, "but it sure will seem like it."

Maybe that's the way with the cold weather. Maybe I'm exaggerating these annoying little inconveniences. For instance, the toe in Young Son's winter boots sprung a leak. Nothing serious, but since he's growing like a cabbage it's silly to buy *him* new gear at the end of the season. So I traded boots with him. After all, he walks to and from the school bus and spends a lot of time outside. I just scurry from car to door (with cold feet).

The wood supply began to run low, which is no big deal because you just call up and order more, right? Wrong. At forty below no one wants to go out gathering wood and none of the advertised suppliers even answered their phones. So switch on the oil furnace.

Except that the cold weather managed to last longer than expected and the oil level is beginning to get frighteningly low. It's been years since we've had oil delivered, no one has us on their books for credit and it's a week and a half before payday. Somehow no wood and less and less oil makes me feel more and more uncomfortable even when I'm bundled up enough to remain warm.

However! As I wrote to Sis last week, there has been one lovely, joyous, positive aspect of existence. My battered little vehicle on which I lavish so much money, concern and attention has managed to run like a top throughout the siege.

Finally the cold weather lightened up, the ice fog toned down, someone agreed to bring us wood and the oil turned out to be not quite as low as I had imagined. A new day dawned, I could see the light at the end of the tunnel!

That morning as we rolled along the road my trusty, dusty, companion of exactly five years *(to the day)* started to shake, rattle and shout. It lost power, the engine uttered sounds reminiscent of Uncle Alfred's thrashing machine and it quietly passed away. As we edged over to the side of the road it gasped, "I've had it." The only light on the dim, dark horizon was the red one on the dash. STOP! it said.

Son was right, those boots are cold for walking.

Oh, well. Some days are better than others, but this is definitely not one of them. More later when I figure out what to do next.

> Much love,
> (The sun is shining, all cannot
> possibly be lost.)
> Edith C.

162

A MEANINGFUL RELATIONSHIP

March 12, 1979

Dear Me!

It has got to be totally and completely ridiculous to be so attached to an automobile that you mourn its passing. When Sis said that parting with their Chevie was like selling a member of the family, I thought, "How disgusting, to get emotional about a mere means of transportation!" Studies which attribute sex and social motives to car choices seem absurd. I pride myself on being immune to such foolishness. My attitude toward automobiles has always been strictly no-nonsense.

At the age of 13 I knew the make and model of every car on the road and could tell you what was stock and what was cherried. (Now I can barely tell a Honda Civic from a pick-up truck.) The day I turned 16 I passed my driver's license test behind the wheel of a 1937 4-door Dodge sedan with a tricky clutch and a shifting rod that took two hands to maneuver. It was Mom's car, not mine. (It was older than I was.)

I had no qualms about that test, though. Dad had taught me to back as fast as I could go forward, stop my right front tire on a dime (or as close to it as possible) and park in two smooth motions. Driving was serious business. (I was the most sedate hotrodder on the road.) To me cars have always been machines meant to take you from one place to another. Nothing more.

Nothing more, except that the car of my dreams was a brand new pink and white Eldorado Cadillac convertible with a horn that played "It's Cherry Pink and Apple Blossom White." It was to be lovely, melodic, graceful, unique, breathtaking, eye catching and have class. Everything a car should be.

Well, I didn't get a car at all for almost twenty years. Reality made some in-roads into my world during that time and buying my first car was a big responsibility. I studied, read, sampled, drove, weighed, calculated and considered. In fact, I considered every car in this town. Then I saw it! Da dum! Just like in the movies. It was love at first sight. We were meant for each other.

It was a perfect size for my needs. It was stately, unusual, attractive, sensible, sturdy, spacious, capable, charming and strong. The ideal car. All right, all right, so it was really a funky little battered-up crab apple green cracker box with several dents and a radio that only worked when you parked in front of a station's transmitter. It guzzled gas, drank almost as much oil and visited my friendly mechanic more often than the budget could handle.

True, all true, but for years we went almost everywhere together. When it was down I was down. I understood it's idiosyncracies (and too often made allowances for its shortcomings). Many were the dreams hatched and secrets said aloud in the safe silence of that dark vinyl interior. We went through a lot together and always did our best to keep each other going. We were friends.

Now I'm on my own. I've got this other car, but it's just a car—a straightforward, no-nonsense means of transportation. Foolish or not, I liked it better the other way.

me

NICER NAGGING

March 5, 1979

Dear Nancy FNTCVV,

Oh, how I envy your graphic talent! I miss those phone messages with spider webs draped from letter to letter and lady bugs perched on daisies. Well I recall a particular note that ended with, "Have a nice weekend!" Lively letters danced across the page enticing me to do the same. It seems to me that only you can make an alphabet bow and twirl. Your quickly penned, "Good Morning, Edee" was always enough to make a grey day glitter. I'll bet your grocery list is worth framing.

Then there's me. No matter how carefully I copy some genius's words of wisdom, my scrawl makes the most quotable quotes look like gobbledygook. I'd like to leave some sparkly little reminders about the house for myself and others, but when I try, the missiles inevitably back fire.

If *you* jotted down, "Please remove both ends of all cans and squash them flat before placing them in garbage can" it would look like a cheerful invitation. As it is, when I penned those words laboriously on a 5" x 8" card and even added a flower (just like you taught me) the response was, "Mother! How could you write something so disgusting and put it out in plain view where just *anyone* can see it?"

Try as I might I cannot see anything off-color about that message. (Although if you tip your head a bit the chrysanthemum does look like a rotten banana peel stuck to a apple core.)

If only I had some small degree of artistic talent, I could tip toe about the premises tacking up pretty posters such as:

"Edith, get back to your desk. Emptying the slop bucket and vacuuming the rug are not valid excuses for missing a deadline."

Over the fruit bowl would go:

"An apple a day keeps the doctor away, but more than one is unhealthy. It incurs the wrath of the systematic shopper and budget balancer. Beware!"

For the refrigerator door:

"You *are not* hungry. You're just bored. Go *do* something. There are fewer calories in shoveling snow than eating a piece of cheese."

At the wood stove:

"If you're cold, don't put a log on the fire, put a sweater on you and go split or carry wood."

Next to the furnace switch:

"Vacuuming, sweeping, dusting and mopping generate heat. If it seems cold in here you must need something to do. Get busy."

Where we stand to look out at the outdoor thermometer:

"Cold keeps the Northland comfortably populated with hardy and unique specimens. If we wanted warm weather and carbon copies we could live in downtown L.A."

On my own personal bulletin board:

"Out of the mouths of babes (even teenaged ones) oft times come gems. So why don't you listen more carefully. Often."

"You can do whatever you want to do. It's up to *you*."

"The only trouble with dealing with the opposite sex is that they're all men."

and last but by no means least:

"All is not lost—Friday's payday."

However, since I lack the flair for making things look fancy, I'm left to pine and reminisce about the works of Nancy.

> Ever so seriously,
> Sincerely,
> Edee

WE DO THIS
FOR RECREATION?

March 19, 1979

Dear Mom and Dad,

I had a theory that I was going to spice up this winter's correspondence with monthly progress reports on the development of my skiing skills, but it appears that a yearly up-date will be sufficient.

So far my big accomplishment for the winter 78-79 is that I've mastered the rope tow. Believe me, that is no incidental victory. Riding a rope tow is slightly more difficult and definitely more frightening than holding onto the end of a rubber hose and being slowly (with frequent sudden jerks) pulled up from the 15th to the 58th story of the Empire State Building where you are expected to let go and leap to safety. (Knowing you've got the entire process under control is somewhat reassuring—to say the least.)

Last year I was just as terrified of slithering up the hill as I was of sliding down. This year I can casually attach myself to that mini-conveyor and get yanked up the hill just as if I knew what I was doing. What a thrill! (What a relief!)

However, what comes up must go down and that's the hard part. I *have* progressed a little. I've gotten past uff, eek! plop (which translates: move, panic, sit). I can now occasionally remain semi-upright for a reasonable amount of time and slow down using any number of relatively orthodox maneuvers. Sometimes I even crash! when my courage exceeds my skill (which isn't often).

I have been persistent though. I can tell—I hurt. In fact, the location of my pains is probably the best indication of my increased ability. The sore part of my person this season is the top of my lap rather than the bottom.

Our household pursues this fascinating sport for restful relaxation and recreation. At least that's what we tell ourselves. We bound out of bed early each weekend morning, load the car with folk, fodder and gear, drive for 1/2 an hour, empty car of same, bundle up and. . . .

Taking our courage in hand—we cram our feet into bright-colored plastic trash compactors that cut off circulation, cause cramping and pain (the only respite being that eventually numbness sets in and you forget you have feet).

Then we travel up and down the mountainside, slipping, sliding, falling and crashing until every bone, muscle and fiber of our being aches. Our cheeks burn from the cold, our noses run and our eyes sting. At the end of the day even the best hot doggers stumble into the lodge looking as if they had just crawled across a cold Sahara to utter a last gasp. As they collapse they stammer weakly, "Gawd!!! That was great!"

We do this for fun, I keep telling myself. That is why I could just barely crawl out of bed this morning. My legs are so sore I need a rope tow to get from the house to the car. I did without coffee and lunch today because the breakroom is one flight up and it hurts when I bend my knees.

However, there is one definite bonus to this regime for an often exasperated parent in a lively, loud and energetic 3-teen family. It's 8:30 p.m. at this moment and as I write this all is calm and quiet on the homefront. Numbers 1, 2 and 3 are all sound asleep. Another night I would really enjoy such silence and stillness, but tonight I think I'll just sign off and go to bed for some restful relaxation.

Think snow,
Dee

FEVERISHLY YOURS

Dear Sis,

Hey! Do you realize it's spring? You probably do. I guess it even looks like spring down there, doesn't it. Therefore, if anyone in your area exhibits attitudes of restlessness, daydreaming, neglected obligations, inappropriate inclinations, reluctance to roll out and rise to routine tasks, short temper, distractability and general anxiety you can dismiss the problem as "spring" fever.

Spring fever has a rather romantic air about it. The sufferer is sympathetically regarded as smitten, sensitive and prone to sweet sentimentality. The ailment reeks of flowers, love, poetry, fluttery birds and lying on one's back in the clover gazing in a daze at the magic of clouds drifting slowly across bright blue sky.

So how come at the same time of year when we up here are overwhelmed with the same symptoms we are branded as having succumbed to *"cabin"* fever? The implications of that disease being that we've gone bonkers, that we're not tough enough to withstand the rigors of the regime we've chosen, not sensible enough to manage our lives so as to avoid sensory deprivation.

What I don't understand is how people who all week long leave the house 30 minutes after slipping out of the sheets, work a full day, do errands, buzz home long enough to catch a quick bite to eat before dashing off to attend a meeting or class or to deliver a child to any number of activities; then on the weekends attend a respectable array of the umpteen cultural events offered, socialize with friends, ski, swim, run, dance, haul wood, shovel snow and write home can find time to catch cabin fever. We're just clever, I guess.

It's spring up here too, you know. Daytime temperatures have been above zero quite regularly. A quick perusal of the local climatological data of years gone by indicates that the coldest it could get between now and the end of the month would be about minus forty degrees. (That's -40° on March 30, 1944.) The end of March has clocked in at 51 above too so we have a wide range to choose from. That's nice. It isn't any fun to be too sure of things. Last week we also passed the halfway mark with daylight. Now we've more light than night.

Of course, we don't have any crocuses bursting through the rich brown earth to herald the season, but I did see some dirt the other day. (To be perfectly honest I must admit it had been dumped on top of the snow and was not peeking through.) For the life of me I cannot figure out where anyone found dirt at this time of year or why they were wasting it. If it had been my dirt I would have gathered it carefully into a container, put a cutting in it and placed it under the grow light. (See we *too* can plant at this time of year.)

Back to my protest. I demand equal rights! Why should spring fever in California be smiled upon and the same season silliness be considered an affliction when it occurs in Alaska? I maintain that it is *SPRING* fever that attacks us at the dreary end of winter. To prove this I'm going to rush right out and start my garden this very minute. That is I'm going to plow through the snow and pour ashes on the frozen compost. Up here that's an excellent beginning.

Fervently yours,
me

OUT OF THE BAG

April 2, 1979

Dear Sis,

My cars, the children and their cats all seem to have an incredible capacity to complicate my existence. This particular lady likes her world to be controllable. The seven "C's" are definitely not that. They fade in and out, group and regroup faster than I can count.

Last time the mother cats multiplied I swore we would never allow it again, and for these many cold months it has been an easy threat to uphold. Recently, though, the times and temperatures changed. Fade in on a confrontation scene.

"Your cat got out last night." I announce with considerable concern and distress.

"Is she gone?" He gasps.

"Oh, no." I utter carefully. "She *got out.*"

"Oh!" He exclaims with a happy grin. *"Got out."* With a paternal shrug and a satisfied nod he struts expectantly across the floor to warm his backside at the fire.

"Yes, *got out.*" I reply testily, adding quickly, "But only for a *short* while."

"Oh." Comes his crestfallen reply.

"Muh! Ther!" Sounds a cry from upstairs. "She was out *at least* half an hour." (Someday we should have doors hung on those rooms.)

"Half an hour!?!" He chimes eagerly. "Which was it? Fifteen minutes? Or half an hour?"

Communication is my field, I think, as I shift from one foot to another, saying slowly, "Well, she was out for somewhere between 15 and 30 minutes."

"Which one!" He insists.

Ah, yes, which one, I consider silently. Just how long was she out there? Not how many minutes, but how much time did she have to roam about? Did she or didn't she find what she was looking for? Will we or won't we? How should I know? I'm a people!

Mother's are supposed to *know* these things. Mothers aren't

170

considered to *know* anything really but they're supposed to have all the answers when the questions get tough. What use are mothers if they can't accurately assess just how long it takes to. . . .

"Mom!" He asks suddenly. "How long does it take to make kittens?"

(Oh, good heavens. How the _____. . . .)

"Sixty days!" comes a shout from the second floor.

"Oh, wow! That's just a couple of months! That's not as long as I thought. I can hardly wait. Suuuper! Kittens!"

Sigh. Smile and relax. Maybe it's just as well that we never have hung doors on those rooms upstairs. The higher-ups can be useful resources at times. It's easier to answer a question when you understand what's being asked.

Perhaps the problem with my cars, cats and children is one of numbers—there's only one of me.

> Much love from your
> One and Only
> Big Sis

TECHNICOLOR BLACKMAIL

April 9, 1979

Dear Sharron,

We had some funny weather here awhile ago. Funny as in mushy and warm in March. In the midst of it I started a letter to you which said:

> "The world is really beginning to behave like spring and I'm getting a bit panicky. I'm not ready. I haven't yet successfully adjusted to winter and I just hate to leave a project before I've mastered it. These slushy days of 40° above are worrisome.

> "Oh, I enjoy the melt. It's always entertaining to watch the terrain subside. Our subdivision turns into slush-city and each trip in or out is fraught with uncertainty. Will we sink? Should we drive or swim? Etc."

Well, that letter got set aside and so did the pleasant weather. By the time I received your letter *and the pictures* it was snowing. The roads were iced over again and danger had shifted back from slurp to slick.

This is a strange time of year for us in the woods. Downtown the open spaces, pavement, people, traffic and snow removal make it possible for ice and snow to disappear rather regularly. However, in our private territory, trees block out the sun, the only traffic is squirrels skimming from tree to tree and domestic snow removal came to a screeching halt when the roof supply of precipitation descended upon the walk.

Our territory is blanketed with deep, solid, serious snow long after the rest of the world gets damp and dry. So our first step into spring is a ping-pong between temperatures (slush-slick, slush-slick) and settings (snow-soot, snow-soot).

As I said, in the midst of this the pictures arrived. If I didn't trust you implicitly. If I wasn't absolutely certain you harbor basically kind thoughts toward me. If I didn't know you have utmost concern for my mental health and happiness, I'd accuse you of malicious intent.

I'll concede that you might not have been exhibiting abject cruelty, but you weren't exactly too subtle either. In one letter you promise not to barrage me with written requests that I travel south for a visit and in the next envelope, true to your vow, there is no mention whatsoever of travel plans, but there is:

(1) One full frame photo of a fluffy deep-yellow acacia tree so sharply in focus that each of those furry little balls threaten to drop off in my lap.

(2) One picture of a pink plum tree in full flower against a background of lush green well-leafed deciduous trees.

(3) And, the clincher (labeled "view from my sewingroom window"), a sunlit spray of cherry blossoms close enough to tickle my nose.

Sharron, the view from my workroom window at this precise moment is a magnificent silver icicle and a pile of wood that needs to have the snow swept from it before it can be restacked.

I do not for one minute think you were boasting or bragging. I also do not for one minute think you were really just trying out the new camera. If that was all you were doing why didn't you send me a still life of dried bananas and twigs? I do appreciate the invitation, be it ever so silently spoken, but I can't leave right now. One of these days *our* trees will burst into spring and I simply must be here to watch the season unfold.

See you soon, or eventually at least.

Dee

TALLY TIME

April 16, 1979

Dear Auntie Carolyn,

Snow bunnies are drifting in, due back momentarily and overdue and with them comes—*the question*. What returnees toss off as a casual Alaskan version of "How-de-do?" causes remainees to take cold, calm scrutinizing inventory of recent months. *The question* is—"How was your winter?"

We need standards, of course, in order to be able to address ourselves to that issue. Of course the standards vary. If your business is pumping and thawing, a good winter is plenty of 50° below. A more popular plus point would be no frozen pipes at all. This could cause economic distress for the aforementioned.

One person's plus is another **one's minus**.

For people in general, it seems to me, it's a good winter if you've got a job, indoors, you enjoy it and it pays well. It's nice if the indoors is relatively warm, not routinely overheated and has windows which face south, but that's asking a bit much.

It's even better if you don't need to have a job, but can still eat and maintain a warm snug place to do your thing. (If that's the case you're probably under 12 and don't think a whole lot about the pros and cons of winter anyway.)

It's a good winter if you don't run out of oil, wood or electricity, or if you do you can replenish the supply easily. In other words, if subzero temperatures do not find you lugging logs, lying on your back under the house putting heat tape on frozen fuel lines or balancing on a wind-swept roof replacing a rotten stove pipe. It's a good winter if your warmth flows smoothly.

It's a remarkably good winter if your means of transportation remains functional throughout. Especially if it does so without large transfusions of money or repeated applications of personal frozen-fingered attention.

It has been a fortunate season indeed when you get to soggy streets without having slid off slick ones into a ditch, without having been back-bumped by someone who didn't adequately plan ahead and with no mechanical difficulty that strands you somewhere you don't want to be on the one day you ventured out without dressing for an emergency.

It's a blessing to be noted if all season long you and yours manage no major injury from slipping on slick streets or steep slopes. Count plus points for minimal power outages occurring at convenient hours, for record breaking lows of ice fog, for record breaking highs of snow fall (provided it occurs regularly and in moderate amounts).

However, we allow no celebration for ridiculous abnormalities like days when it's safe to wear shoes rather than boots, a season-long scarcity of subzero temperatures, mushy days in February, and so forth. Though mellow, mild, manageable winter months might sound desirable to those in less challenging climates it has been scientifically proven that moderate conditions in Fairbanks, Alaska, are unhealthy.

The fact is, in this town a good winter is a bad winter, for the inhabitants only feel solid satisfaction in having survived a respectably difficult siege. So the usual interchange between tan and pale goes something like this: "How was your winter?" "Just awful." "Oh, that's nice." "And yours?" "Quite pleasant." "Gee, that's too bad."

All things are relative and my winter was relatively awful (therefore good). How about my relatives?

> Your loving niece,
> Edith C.

MAGICAL MIDNIGHT MATINEE

Dear Mom and Dad,

Driving home the other night, hunched over the steering wheel, scrunched up to the windshield and craning my neck to peer out at the undulating sparkles of a particularly active aurora I was struck by the fact that I haven't ever tried to describe this incredible vision to you.

Watching the miles-wide swath of light snake across the black velvet sky in slow, smooth gyrations I began to wonder why I've never said much about it. Then as the ballet of shape surprised me by turning itself inside out and appearing in a new spot as a new form it occurred to me that there isn't a whole lot to *say* about the northern lights. You've got to see them to appreciate them. See them and hear them.

Some people claim the lights don't make noise. Others insist that they do. One thing is for sure, if you're outdoors in a quiet area while you're watching a display it's easy to hear (or imagine) a sort of tingling noise, a vibration kind of quiver like the hum of an unplucked quitar string plus an ever so subtle snap-crackle-pop. Like the first time you ever heard Rice Crispies and thought they were a grown-up put-on so didn't know whether there was really a sound at all. That's it.

We've an imposing composer in our midst who created a symphony which includes a tribute to our visual masterpiece of the sky. If we had an amphitheater where the orchestra could play Gordon Wright's Symphony in Ursa Major out under the stars the music just might induce the mystical mural to materialize.

Actually, that's not a practical plan, because it wouldn't be warm enough to play outdoors when it was dark enough to see the aurora and it wouldn't be dark enough to see when it was warm enough to play. Might be fun to try though.

This idea popped into my head because the first time I ever saw an aurora we were oohhing and aahhing with a large group of newcomers to the Great Land when someone announced, "The Geophysical Institute makes that, you know."

To appreciate this you need to know that the Geophysical Institute is a branch of our local University where many charming and intelligent people gather to try to figure things out. From the outside the establishment (a solid, sensible block of concrete) is assumed to be full of people who know a great deal.

On the inside it's obvious that the inhabitants are actually people who know enough to know they don't know and are busy trying to find out. Which is by way of saying that the symphony probably has as much chance of "making" the fancy sky lights as the scientists do.

Once I considered various drawings and photographs of the aurora as presents for you, but I ended up deciding you just don't get the picture from pictures. You've got to experience the phenomenon to appreciate it. It's the spine-tingling, mindboggling wonder of the apparition that makes the "electrical discharge in the upper atmosphere" such a thrilling sensation, and that just can't be put down on paper. Looks as if you're going to have to come on up and see for yourself.

Yours in natural neon,
Dee

BUT I'M NOT SURE WHY

April 30, 1979

Sarah!

How is spring in Norway? Is the climate and terrain there similar to here? It sure looks as if it should be when you glance at a globe. You are just as near "the top" on one side as we are on the other.

Speaking of near the top. Jill and I just returned from the Glacier Stampede. What a trek! I hesitate to suggest you undertake the adventure someday for fear you might curse me the entire way and suspect that torture was my motive.

Eight years ago I made the trip and it's taken me all this time to forget enough of the pain and agony that I could consider doing it again. Consider, baloney, I was compelled. I was consumed with determination to travel that trail and it's just as well too, because I don't know what else could get one up that incline.

I'll record for you our observations in case you ever do decide to go. Then at least you can't claim we didn't warn you.

The first hardship is getting out of bed super early on a Saturday morning. Next comes a sleepy drive of a couple hundred miles from the soggy spring-sodden streets of our town right back to winter. In the mountains we were met with other people of similar intent and more snow than we've had here all winter, but the day was sunny so who should complain. We should.

The snow was slick, our skis slipped and we squinted for 8 warm, laborious miles. Up the valley we plodded surrounded by mountain peaks, snow dunes, distant crevasses and unbelieveable expanses of undulating snow, shadowed and highlighted with intriguing patterns. Continuously I thought of a dear friend's response to her husband's oft-repeated plea that she cross-country ski with him in order to witness such wonders.

Her plaintive reply. (My sentiments exactly.) "When *I* ski, all I ever see is the tips of my skis." To which daughter adds, "and the bottom of the person in front of me."

The designated destination is tent city on a mountainside. Why does any sensible outdoor's person lug a pack 8 miles into the wilderness to pitch a tent two feet from another? The socializing is warm, but that's all that offers much heat. You tend to feel chilly when standing, sitting and sleeping on 500 feet of ice.

Since the trip up netted us severe sunburns, the frightening white-out which masked the return trip was almost a blessing. It made an excellent sunscreen. In fact, it made a pretty good everything screen. A white-out is an incredible experience. It takes courage to slide down a hillside into nothingness.

At the end of the trail we emerged, blistered on feet and face, backpack bruised, muscle sore and bone weary. We rode in silence, dazed and dangerously near sleep. Each sorted images of what we'd just endured. At one point came the quiet comment, "Even so, I'm glad we went, but I'm not sure why."

That's just it. We recommend it, not because in retrospect the accomplishment was glorious, but because for some unknown reason it feels good to have done it.

Glaedelig Jul! That's Merry Christmas in Danish. It's the closest I could get to saying HURRY HOME!!! in Norwegian.

We miss you,
Edee

BLESS THIS SHELL

May 7, 1979

Dear Cindy,

How are Alaskan houses different? That, my dear sweet niece, is an interesting question. First of all, it isn't really the multi-layered windows, the extra insulation, the cold weather entry or the emphasis on heating and heatability that distinguish our domiciles. It isn't the fact that houses up here might be made of log or that many are homemade. What really makes a difference between our houses and yours is that those tend to be *finished products* meant for moving into and these are *organic*—they grow.

Certainly homegrown houses exist in the Lower 48 and I'm sure we must have some *relatively* completed projects in these parts, but by and large, *you* expect a house to just sit there and be lived in while we know full well it will evolve. That is, it will change and grow as we do, though never fast enough or finished enough to suit us.

My first recollection of *this* "house" is of walking up and down our dusty dirt road comparing all the acres available. I recall agonizing over location, fussing about which trees to fell, fighting with a chain saw and finally planting the stakes in a place where trees could be deleted with an axe and a Swede saw. Thus I determined where to put down roots.

After several months, when the carpenters and my money were gone, I was left with a very primitive shell of what would someday be our home. The interior stud walls had no siding on them, but those bare boundaries attested to the fact that ours was about to become the world's smallest 4 bedroom house.

Exterior walls and ceilings were stuffed with insulation covered with clear plastic, for kitchen "cabinets" I nailed together left-over 2 x 6's and balanced plywood on them. (No Blazo boxes for me.) They wobbled. I nailed them to the wall, thus upgrading their status to that of "built-in." We took up residence in a habitat that might be barely considered inhabitable.

Actually such incidental details were overshadowed by the fact that though the agreed upon had been accomplished we were without a livingroom and a door (there was a hole in the wall, of course, but my dream of a handcrafted door to put into the opening had long since sunk into the driveway as extra loads of gravel.)

All that and more are memories made palatable by the passage of time. Much has changed since that first sinking realization that to bring a dreamhouse to reality many a nightmare must be endured.

Years later, as a carpenter fancified the kitchen, I turned the 2 x 6's into a mock-up of a built-in couch. When she created the "real" couch those same boards took on the shape of bedroom storage shelves. At long last a closet was constructed and with great pride and pleasure I relegated the kitchen/couch/closet lumber to a walkway.

So it goes, cutting back the old leaves to encourage new growth. Other houses get older, ours gets better with age. I'm so glad you're coming to visit this summer. I think you'll understand better once you see some of our houses that have actually sprouted wings.

Much love,
Aunt Edee

THE URGE TO EMERGE

May 14, 1979

Dear Sis,

Oh, my goodness gracious, it's hard to stay indoors when it's spring! I feel like a crocus, encased in damp, cold, confining earth (the household chores) pushing to emerge into the sunshine.

This is miserable! On days when I'm confined to lighted, heated, fan-droning buildings and nowhere near a window I don't suffer so badly. Here, at my desk, looking out at the spruce trees, blue sky, puffs of filmy white clouds and sunshine, I'm in pain. Even the insects look inviting.

Fairbanks is usually a splendid place for a procrastinator. When time comes to pay bills, write home or clean house it's easy to feel noble about bundling up and braving the elements to do something else. (It doesn't really matter what you escape to do as long as it gets you away from what you're supposed to be doing.)

Not only that, since few of us indulge in enough exercise during winter months we can justify time out from obligations to go cross-country skiing, for a long walk, to swim, bowl or even dance. Considering the fact that cabin fever is an actual threat to our mental health we can legitimately leave the premises for a midday peak at the glowing mountains, a life-saving chat with a friend or a sociable hot toddy in a friendly bar. All in the interests of survival.

That's wintertime indulgence. Inescapable adversity makes conscience easing easy. With spring the situation is definitely different. Like hungry chicks stepping from eggs, like bees bursting from the hive in search of sustenance, like children through the school door at the end of a day the overwhelming desire is to be out in the open and *free!*

Consequently, these days, no matter what you decide to do, be it spade up the garden plot, dig channels for run-off, pick up garbage, sweep away soot, chop wood, etcetera, you know in your heart that the real reason you are so diligently tending to tasks is that you cannot manage to force yourself to remain indoors.

180

How can I, with a clear conscience, apologize for my tardy reply to your letter with the explanation that I simply had to move the greenhouse, wash the car, clean up the yard or do anything else that puts me outdoors. I know better.

A colleague mentioned to me at lunch last week that he was about to spend all his spare time gathering the umpteen cords of wood necessary to heat his house next winter. How efficient! I thought. How diligent! What a solid, responsible householder!

Then today as I sat here gazing out at my woods and my wood pile forcing myself to pound the typewriter wishing I could go rake up sawdust, build another wooden walkway or do almost anything that would put me out rather than in, it dawned on me.

He's not noble, efficient, organized or anything of the sort. He wasn't bragging. He was confessing. He must be playing hookey from whatever he's supposed to be doing—an indoor chore I'll guarantee. I'm not fooled one bit.

I'd better sign off and write to the folks so they won't assume I disappeared with the snow, although I'd much rather go out and. . . .

Oh well,
Your Shackled Sis

KEEP ME POSTED

May 21, 1979

Dear Chris,

You know, I really cannot relate to the fact that you don't like to write letters. How could we both issue from the same set of circumstances and differ so drastically on such an important point?

For me letter writing is essential, right up there with inhaling, exhaling and eating. In fact, at times I worry that if I don't put down on paper what's happening in my heart and my head I just might disappear.

Then there's you who apparently never fully grasped a pencil's intended use. You ought to try it! Letter writing is so safe, so satisfying, such a marvelous outlet. (Some of my more romantic moments were strictly chaperoned by the postal service.)

One of the assets of letter writing is the opportunity to take back what you've said before it's reached the eyes of the intended beholder. Many's the letter I've written and re-written or written, re-read and de-written. Many's the time I've wished it were as easy to shut my mouth as it is to scrumple up printed pouting. Seeing what you've said before it's delivered is the ultimate count to ten.

Perchance persistent letter writers are actually cowards. I find it much easier to "say" something in print than to state my views in person. Not seeing the response of the recipient spares one the gut-wrench of experienced exposure.

For me letter writing is a way of life. Considering options, making plans, finding solutions, even dreaming of future accomplishments are all done in the form of letters—mailed or mental. Often my "letters" never reach paper let alone the addressee. I always carry on monologues in my head while going about the business of everyday existence. If everyone received each tome I composed while driving or doing the dishes I suspect all my friends and family would have unlisted addresses in self-defense.

Alas, I must admit that my own excellent record of regular, lengthy, newsy correspondence is not motivated so much by a need to communicate as by survival instinct. So to proselytize (which I disapprove of) is inappropriate, indeed.

My true desire in trying to interest you in the enterprise of putting pen to paper is a selfish need to hear from you and know what's going on in your life.

Mine not to reason why. I love you. I choose to accept you as you are, including your aversion to written communication. Well-spaced telephone calls will have to suffice. (Gee, it was nice to talk to you last week.)

I would like to say, however, and I admit it's meant as a bit of a nudge: When you do write, you do write exceptionally fine letters. Please do write, at least occasionally.

Until the next phone call, or the postman issues a recall on your envelopes and sends one of them my way. Remember I'm thinking of you.

Much love,
Dee

MEMORIAL DAY

May 29, 1979

Dear me,

The world just turned upside down and inside out. In my Camelot, Pollyana, rose-tinted Fairbanks, Alaska, cold, cruel, senseless violence has shattered all illusions. The naive "bad-things-only-happen-elsewhere" attitude that so many of us harbor just received an eye-opening, gut-wrenching update.

Billy Berry has been shot and killed. Gentle, philosophical, sympathetic William just got blown apart by a crazy man.

"How can this happen!?!" We all exclaim.

How? He cared. He stuck his neck out. He walked into a potentially dangerous situation because he knew someone was in distress. A watch dog Bill Berry was not. His inclinations were totally nonviolent. There was never ever even any harshness to his voice, much less his manner. Reassurance, not protection, was his gift. What animal suggests an appropriate metaphor? Bill would have known.

Bill had been a quiet observer of animals since early childhood. Ever unobtrusive, his observation of wildlife was not so disruptive as the click of a camera. Bill sketched and took notes as he watched the creatures that fascinated him.

When he drew or painted animals each muscle, motion and hair was represented with meticulous accuracy. He was an artist with a thorough knowledge of anatomy. The attention to detail and reality of his drawings was intriguing, especially so, since some of his subjects were unicorns and mammoths.

Bill's knowledge of biology was balanced by a world of fantasy. His head held a store of beings, places and stories waiting in line to be set loose to roam on paper or in print.

Bill's animals were totally realistic, though inclined to do unanimal things like dance and have picnics to which they carry honey pots created by Liz Berry. Yet Bill Berry people are a bit fanciful—too good to be true.

On party posters, "the" magic mural and private personal greeting cards, Bill drew prettier, happier, livelier, more nicely formed human beings than life has ever offered.

This shaggy, sweatshirted, huggable sage left us drawings, paintings, books, sculptures and decorations on pottery. The world according to Bill Berry is delightful to look at, charming to experience and speaks of touching and caring.

The emptiness in my heart and bewilderment in my head is slowly filling with fond memories of his warmth. The anguished cry of WHY? that has interrupted each day since his death is admonished by the answer, "Because he cared."

His loss hurts so much and so many because he was such a caring person; and because he cared he is no longer with us, except in the spirit of all the enchantment he left behind. Each memory of and bit of work by Bill nudges us. "Open up your hearts to each other—*now,*" he urges.

(Oh, Bill, how much we miss you!)

At the time of Bill Berry's death he was working on the illustrations for this book. Five of the twenty planned had been completed. Typical of Bill's precision and attention to detail, he had many working sketches for reference. These are a few examples of his "field sketches" of Edee Rohde.

VERY STRAIGHT
LINE TO INCISORS —

DEEP FOLD TO
OUTER CORNER OF LID —
ALSO TO LID ITSELF —

(MOMMY)
MORE EVEEANA —
MAR 29, '79 —

A CHARACTERISTIC
GRIN (NOT ACCURATE
HERE) — LOWER LIP
UP OVER UPPER TEETH —

EVEEKO —

OR JUST
CAT CURLED
UP ON
HEARTH
OR SOMETHING

DRAWKNIFE —

NOTES ON EDSE –
FEB 24, 1'79 –
(MEMORY)

STRAIGHT
FOREHEAD-NOSE
LINE –
JAW PROFILE ?

LINE OF EYELID
CHARACTERISTIC –
DARK, VERY
DISTINCT –
(LARGE-EYE LOOK)

UPPER TEETH
& GUM LINE SHOWS
IN SMILE – (NOTE PRO-
JECTING LINE OF
MOUTH IN PROFILE)
BUT UPPER LIP
NOT ESPECIALLY
SHORT –
SHAPE OF LIPS ?

186

IT'S THE PEOPLE

Well, Bill,

You asked me to do a letter on the good things about our lifestyle, "especially the people." You said, "coping is easy to poke fun at and get a smile from, but one more time before you sign off it would be good to summarize the special things about our world, especially the people."

Especially the people.

Since it amused you to realize that my letters were created right as they happened and you were always so quick to see the gentle humor in every situation, I do believe you would have appreciated the irony in the fact that your death provided the inspiration for this next to the last letter.

I've rolled your request around in my head. I've re-read the letters to see what I've left out, especially about the people. I've edged closer and closer to deadline, but then my editors are very tolerant and understanding, especially good people.

In my work-it-out-on-paper, write-it-out-to-figure-it-out fashion I've been trying to understand why we believe there are more, better people in the Northland than elsewhere.

What do we value when it comes to people? What do we mean when we say there are quality folks up here? We admire energy, creativity, vigor, caring, warmth, generosity, individuality, tolerance and oh so many other aspects of being. We treasure the acceptance, encouragement, moral support and concern we experience from others. We thrive on this and therein lies the answer.

I had coffee with Liz today. We talked about you, of course, and then driving away from that place of so many serious discussions, sweaty saunas, lively dancing parties, tasty pot lucks, silent sketch sessions, wearying work parties and general gatherings of good people the answer came to mind.

Good people *create* good people. Good people foster the growth of each other. There is goodness everywhere in everyone. People who don't seem to have flowered into fine individuals often just don't have the opportunity, don't know how yet, or don't have the courage.

In our community it doesn't take quite as much courage to have courage because there is so much encouragement and acceptance from others who are also busy evolving into the best they can possibly be. This is a growing kind of place. Vegetables get extra big. People get extra fine.

Words, words, words. What do I mean? When bad things happen, we rally together. When one is down others notice and take time to offer support. When you're up others rejoice in your success. When you're different people admire rather than admonish, or at the very least accept and try to understand. It comes naturally to live at being the best kind of person we can up here because becoming is accepted and expected.

Maybe so far away from "the rest of the world" we each try just a little bit harder to achieve our potential because we're all we've got. We set good examples for each other. You be the best *you*, you can be and I'll, in turn, be the very best me. Don't stop at being the best at what you do, go on to become the finest possible you.

You know what. *You* certainly did set a very good example. Good people create good people. That was it, Bill. Why aren't you here so I can tell you what I discovered and see if you agree?

me

SWAN SONG

June 11, 1979

Dear Readers,

It's time to travel on. There is so much to see and do in this land and in this world that it's hard to find time to experience enough. The fascination, excitement and satisfaction of being alive is so enjoyable it's possible to get distracted along the way and partake too long of one accomplishment, event or location, thereby missing others.

Places I haven't been yet are beckoning me. Things I haven't done yet are begging to be approached. If I stay snug and secure here I'll never know the places or the pleasures or the people I've intended to find. I was not meant to remain anywhere very long.

I'm leaving here all right, but not by selling this funky unfinished house which has begun to be quite charming in spots. This odd shaped, lop-sided, inadequate, humble hut is home and I'm attached to it. It's my root system, but the time has come to branch out in other directions. I've never been to the Brooks Range, the Arctic Ocean, or the Bering Sea, I've yet to raft a river. . . . There are places to visit, people to see, books to write, skills to acquire, ideas to explore, knowledge to gain and it's time to travel on.

Writing the column has become a very important part of my life, from imagining which of my perceptions and experiences might interest others, through recognizing and realizing that I was capable of putting pen to paper, to having strangers and friends comment that they agree with or enjoy what I have had to offer.

I will miss this column immensely: The discipline, the weekly reason to scrutinize our world, the audience, the communication, the satisfaction and pleasure of accomplishing a task, the contact with News-Miner people, but it's ever so nice to move on to new things from what one treasures rather than to leave because a task had lost its allure.

Moving on is what my Alaska is all about. Growing (moving on) is what life is all about. It takes time and space to grow. Up here we have the right kinds of space so it's extremely important that we make good use of our time.

My column was a dream. Having made this dream into a reality it's time to travel toward others. There are always new dreams to conquer, like dragons in a canyon, not to slay, but to tame so they tag along behind as memories, as contributions to the essence of an individual.

Thank you for sharing this dream with me. I hope your dreams are as satisfying and sustaining as this one has been for me.

I remain,
Just me,
Edith C. Rohde

INDEX